50 Early Childhood Strategies for Working and Communicating with Diverse Families

JANET GONZALEZ-MENA

Napa Valley College, Emerita

PEARSON

Merrill
Prentice Hall

Upper Saddle River, New Jersey
Columbus, Ohio

Library of Congress Cataloging-in-Publication Data

Gonzalez-Mena, Janet
  50 early childhood strategies for working and communicating with diverse families /
Janet Gonzalez-Mena.
    p. cm.
  Includes bibliographical references and index.
  ISBN 0-13-188857-9
    1. Children—Services for—United States.   2. Early childhood education—United States.   3. Family
services—United States.   4. Multiculturalism—United States.   I. Title.   II. Title: Fifty early childhood
strategies for working and communicating with diverse families.

HV741.G637 2007
362.70973—dc22

2006044815

Vice President and Executive Publisher: Jeffery W. Johnston
Publisher: Kevin M. Davis
Acquisitions Editor: Julie Peters
Editorial Assistant: Tiffany Bitzel
Senior Production Editor: Linda Hillis Bayma
Production Coordinator: Rebecca K. Giusti, GGS Book Services
Design Coordinator: Diane C. Lorenzo
Cover Designer: Candace Rowley
Cover photo: Tim Gonzalez-Mena
Production Manager: Laura Messerly
Director of Marketing: David Gesell
Marketing Manager: Amy Judd
Marketing Coordinator: Brian Mounts

This book was set in Optima by GGS Book Services. It was printed and bound by Banta Book Group. The cover
was printed by The Lehigh Press, Inc.

Photo Credits: All photos by Tim Gonzalez-Mena.

Pearson Prentice Hall™ is a trademark of Pearson Education, Inc.
Pearson® is a registered trademark of Pearson plc
Prentice Hall® is a registered trademark of Pearson Education, Inc.
Merrill® is a registered trademark of Pearson Education, Inc.

Pearson Education Ltd.
Pearson Education Singapore Pte. Ltd.
Pearson Education Canada, Ltd.
Pearson Education—Japan

Pearson Education Australia Pty. Limited
Pearson Education North Asia Ltd.
Pearson Educación de Mexico, S.A. de C.V.
Pearson Education Malaysia Pte. Ltd.

PEARSON
Merrill
Prentice Hall

10 9 8 7 6 5 4 3 2
ISBN: 0-13-188857-9

Introduction

This practical book provides strategies on partnering with families to support, enhance, and maximize the quality of care and education of young children. Many of the strategies in this book address ideas about how early childhood professionals can create a climate of trust by communicating with family members in a collaborative way. The goal is to create useful, inclusive programs that respect and honor differences in families and individuals. These easy-to-use strategies provide a strong basis for working and communicating productively with families.

Several dilemmas faced me as I sat down to write this book. The first one was the big question of how to organize the book. It had to be practical and easy to use. That meant I had to tease apart subjects that are enormously large and complex. Organizing alphabetically by categories was a way to accomplish that goal. As you read on, you'll see that the complexity still exists, because all the categories are intertwined. As you begin to discern the threads running through all of strategies, you'll see those many small chunks turn into a whole fabric.

FAMILY-CENTERED CARE AND EDUCATION

The threads make patterns. The background pattern is a single concept: *family-centered care and education*. The tendency in the early care and education (ECE) field has been to focus on the child, and indeed some programs in their philosophy statement actually use the words "child-centered programs." This book is based on the idea that you can't ever separate the child from the context of the family. *The child* is a term that has no real meaning, because no child stands alone; the influences of the family are always present. When programs regard those influences as a good thing, they are on their way to becoming family centered. When a program becomes family centered, diversity is a part of the package. You'll see that respecting diversity is a highlight of many of the strategies and is quietly implied in the rest. With diversity comes the idea of equity as well as inclusion, meaning that you have to include everybody. You can't celebrate diversity and then exclude some families from the program because they or their child is too *different*. This book is about including *all* families and their children. It's about honoring diversity, even when it is hard to do so.

WHAT DOES "PARTNERSHIP" REALLY MEAN?

Partnerships are another part of the background pattern. In fact, establishing trust is a key thread, because you can't have a partnership without trust. A partnership is different from merely trying to get families to cooperate with the program and carry out its goals. Involving parents is an approach often taken with that idea in mind. Policymakers learn about how school readiness and academic achievement are strengthened when parents are involved in their children's education. They jump on a bandwagon to teach parents how to help their children carry out the program goals. The parents then learn how to help their children according to the school's way of doing things.

A partnership is different from parent involvement because it implies equity and shared power rather than one side dominating the other. In a partnership, roles and responsibilities may differ, but both sides have rights. At the heart of the partnership lies the welfare of the child. Each partner—family member and teacher—brings different strengths and skills to the union. Partners collaborate rather than issue orders. In a partnership, communication is two-way rather than hierarchical. It takes communication skills to work in partnership. Accordingly, many of the strategies in this book relate to communication. In a partnership, communication is two-way rather than hierarchical. Communication may be very different if the focus of the school is merely about getting parents on board so they can help their children by doing things at home that the school system and educators see as beneficial to readiness or academic achievement.

TRANSFORMATIVE EDUCATION IS THE MODEL

A parent involvement approach is often linked with parent education. The partnership approach is not the same, even though both involvement and education may well be part of it. Certainly, families who are involved in a program are more likely to take their partnership role seriously. Also, ECE professionals have knowledge, experience, and expertise that parents can benefit from; at the same time, parents know their own child, goals, beliefs, values, family traditions, and culture better than anyone else. So the educational model here is *transformative education* rather than the traditional teacher-student, one-way educational approach.

Transformative education is defined as two people or groups coming together and interacting in such a way that both parties learn something and are changed for the better by the interaction.

SOLVING THE NAME DILEMMAS

In addition to organization, another dilemma I faced was what to call the adults who work in early childhood programs. This book takes a wide sweep of early childhood and includes children from birth to 8 years old. Although all adults in these programs could be called teachers, some who work with the youngest children resist that term because they don't *teach*, they *care for*. Others who resist the term *teacher* think of themselves as facilitators of learning and prefer to think of themselves as *educators*. Still other adults who work with children in that age range work out of their homes, not in schools or centers, and call themselves *family child care providers*. Others who work in the homes of the families they serve call themselves *home visitors*. Early childhood education is a complex field, and there is no one name that works for everybody in it.

I also had to figure out a name for the early childhood programs themselves that included all the different forms. A third-grade classroom with a teacher is different from an infant-toddler center with caregivers, yet both fit under a label *early childhood education*. A half-day preschool is different from a kindergarten and also different from a full-day child care program, which is different from a hospital child care center that is open 24 hours a day to serve staff on all shifts.

CARE AND EDUCATION CAN NEVER BE SEPARATED

So what names did I use? I addressed those two dilemmas by changing "early childhood education" to "early care and education" and calling the adults who work in the field *early care and education (ECE) professionals*. Adding the word *care* highlights the idea that care and education can never be separated in the early years. Strategy 11 explains that idea further. So where you see the letters ECE, you have to think care and education—not education alone. That change of wording brings child care programs fully into the picture. Although I used the term *ECE professionals* to label the adults who work with children and their parents in this big variety of programs, I also used other terms, such as *caregiver* or *staff*, depending on whether I meant to include infants and toddlers. Other terms also varied by the focus of the strategy, so sometimes I used *school* and *classroom*, and other times I used *ECE program* and *center*. Sometimes I was aiming more at teachers in school and other times more at staff in programs such as prekindergarten or preschool, infant-toddler programs, early intervention programs, child care, Head Start, Early Head Start, kindergarten, primary, and school-age child care. It's complex, because these programs take place in a variety of environments, including centers, schools, or homes, and some strategies pertain more to one setting than to the others.

In summary, this book is a targeted text that offers practical strategies for partnering with families, creating the trust necessary for true collaboration, and developing programs that include all families and individuals. Of course, at the heart of all these useful strategies lies the welfare of the child.

ACKNOWLEDGMENTS

I would like to thank the following people for helping make this book what it is: Marion Cowee, Lynn Doherty, Tim Gonzalez-Mena, Lisa Lee, Kitty Ritz, Ethel Seiderman, and Joan Symonds. In addition, I wish to thank the following reviewers for their suggestions and insights: Irene Cook, California State University, Bakersfield; Sandi Jessen, Minnesota State University, Mankato; Alycia Maurer, University of Texas, San Antonio; and Lynda Roberts, Cerritos College.

Teacher Preparation Classroom

TEACHER PREP

MERRILL PRENTICE HALL

See a demo at
www.prenhall.com/teacherprep/demo

Your Class. Their Careers. Our Future. Will your students be prepared?

We invite you to explore our new, innovative and engaging website and all that it has to offer you, your course, and tomorrow's educators! Organized around the major courses pre-service teachers take, the Teacher Preparation site provides media, student/teacher artifacts, strategies, research articles, and other resources to equip your students with the quality tools needed to excel in their courses and prepare them for their first classroom.

This ultimate on-line education resource is available at no cost, when packaged with a Merrill text, and will provide you and your students access to:

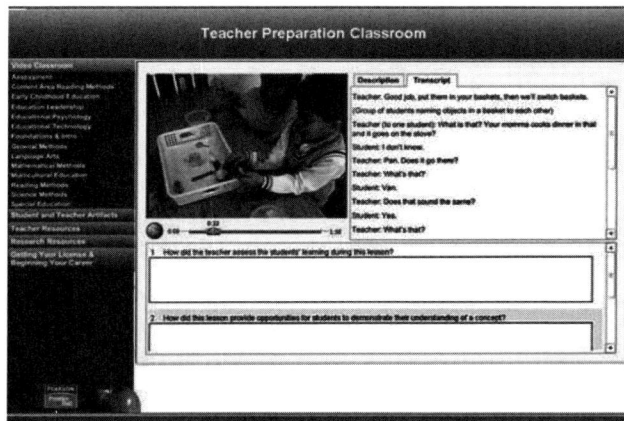

Online Video Library. More than 150 video clips—each tied to a course topic and framed by learning goals and Praxis-type questions—capture real teachers and students working in real classrooms, as well as in-depth interviews with both students and educators.

Student and Teacher Artifacts. More than 200 student and teacher classroom artifacts—each tied to a course topic and framed by learning goals and application questions—provide a wealth of materials and experiences to help make your study to become a professional teacher more concrete and hands-on.

Research Articles. Over 500 articles from ASCD's renowned journal *Educational Leadership*. The site also includes Research Navigator, a searchable database of additional educational journals.

Teaching Strategies. Over 500 strategies and lesson plans for you to use when you become a practicing professional.

Licensure and Career Tools. Resources devoted to helping you pass your licensure exam; learn standards, law, and public policies; plan a teaching portfolio; and succeed in your first year of teaching.

How to ORDER *Teacher Prep* for you and your students:

For students to receive a *Teacher Prep* Access Code with this text, instructors **must** provide a special value pack ISBN number on their textbook order form. To receive this special ISBN, please email: **Merrill.marketing@pearsoned.com** and provide the following information:
- Name and Affiliation
- Author/Title/Edition of Merrill text

Upon ordering *Teacher Prep* for their students, instructors will be given a lifetime *Teacher Prep* Access Code.

Contents

1

ADVOCACY: PARENTS AS ADVOCATES FOR THEIR OWN CHILDREN

RATIONALE

A role for family members that comes naturally to some, but not all, is to advocate for their own child. For those who don't see themselves in this role, it's up to the early childhood professional to help them understand that they have a right to be their child's advocate.

How does a family show that they are advocating for their own child? When a mother comes in to pick up her child at the end of the day and asks the teacher how the day went, she is usually asking about her own child, not about the teacher's day. She wants to know about the other children, but mostly in relation to her own child. When she focuses on her own child, she isn't showing a lack of concern for the rest, or ignoring the teacher's well-being, she is being an advocate for her child.

When family members stand up for their own child in the face of all the others, their attitude may put them in opposition to the professionals whose role is to advocate for the group rather than singling out one child in the group. For example, one family member who comes from a culture where women stay covered up complained about her 4-year-old daughter running around without a shirt on, which was common practice in the preschool on warm days. Another family member who came from a state in the United States where there are hookworms in the soil complained about her child running around barefoot and wanted his shoes left on at all times. Neither request is unreasonable. Yet both requests make it hard on the teacher, first to remember the individual requests and then to carry them out when most of the other children are shirtless and shoeless. It becomes even harder when the two children concerned want to join the crowd and do what the rest of the children are doing. An even more difficult problem arises when a family member whose religion forbids celebration of holidays confronts a teacher whose curriculum is built around holidays and seasons. Why doesn't it seem unreasonable to this family member that the other children be denied their pleasure for the sake of a single child? When the teacher understands that families are advocates for their own children, then the request or demand makes sense.

Although it may seem wrong to change a whole program for one child, think about the idea of including children with special needs in a program or classroom set up for typically developing children. Individualizing can be as important for *all* children and families as it is for those with special needs.

It's important, when thinking about families as advocates for their children, to be fully aware that being a parent is very different from being a teacher. Keeping this fact in mind is vital to working well with families. One difference, according to Lilian Katz, is that families are particularistic—favor their own children over others, have an emotional stake in their children's welfare, are biased in favor of their own children, and put their children's needs first even at the expense of other children's needs. Early childhood education professionals must be universalistic—be concerned about every child in the group without bias, not put any one child first at the expense of the others, and apply skills and resources to each child.

APPROACHES

- Appreciate when parents stand up for their own child. This is a healthy kind of bias, even though it may make your job more difficult. All children need an advocate who takes their side.
- Support families in their role as advocate for their child.

- Help families who don't have strong advocacy tendencies to acquire them. Part of this approach involves asking them about their child on an ongoing basis.
- At the very beginning of your relationship with the family, ask what their goals are for their child. Better yet, ask what their *dreams* are for their child. Erma Bombeck, a humorous author, wrote, "It takes a lot of courage to show your dreams to someone else." That's why forming a relationship and building trust with families is so important! Asking parents about their dreams for their children is an approach that Jean Monroe, national early childhood consultant and trainer based in California, suggests. Parents who discuss their dreams rather than their goals for their child tend to set their sights higher. After you ask, really listen to what they have to say. Make it a point to always listen to them when they talk about their child.
- See the families' natural tendency toward advocacy as something that can be expanded to advocacy for the program in the face of budget cuts, for example. (See Strategy 2, Advocacy: Parents Becoming Advocates for All Children.)
- When the family's advocacy tendencies conflict with your perspective, practice holding their perspective in mind as well as your own. It's a matter of becoming self-aware—observing yourself from a distance even when engaged in an emotional conversation. Keep reminding yourself that it's good that they are advocating for their child.
- Be flexible. Acknowledge that there are whole realms of possibilities in addition to the ways you are comfortable with or have always done things.
- Learn win-win negotiation skills (See Strategy 20.)
- Keep in mind the differences in roles between parent and professional. Your relationship with the child is short term and can end abruptly. You don't have a history or a long-term future. You're not the parent.

Parents who participate in early care and education programs tend to be advocates for their own children, and some go on to become advocates for children in general.

2

ADVOCACY: PARENTS BECOMING ADVOCATES FOR ALL CHILDREN

RATIONALE

Families who start out by advocating for their own children (see Strategy 1) often end up becoming advocates for the group of children of which their child is a member. A natural progression for some families is to focus on their own child and the group or class he or she is in. Some move beyond that to advocating for the school or program. Other families skip all those steps and become advocates for children in general.

The importance of child advocacy is a lesson that many who enter the field of ECE learn, whether they are professionals or parents. Children can't speak for themselves, so adults have to speak for them. When budget cuts come to child care programs, when school districts or state departments of education mandate curriculum that is developmentally inappropriate, culturally inappropriate, or harmful in other ways, who can speak for children? The voices most heard are those of parents—the consumers. Some families are natural advocates and understand the process. They will protest without urging when their children can't get what they need from the powers that be. Other families have to learn to be advocates. They can learn a good deal from those who run and work in the ECE programs their children attend.

Advocacy can start close to home and feel uncomfortable for the professionals at first. For example, a parent or group of parents can push for a change in the program. One example was reported by Jim Greenman (reported in Gonzalez-Mena, 2005a). A group of African American parents got together and told their teachers that they didn't want their children to go outside anymore. The teachers started a parent education campaign to make sure the parents understood the influence of gross motor development on cognition and the importance of fresh air and exercise to health. They continued with the outdoor program. The parents demanded a change. It wasn't until the two sides finally sat down together and the teachers asked the parents what was behind their demand that the true problem came out into the open. It was the sandbox. Children were coming home with sand in their hair, which was causing all kinds of problems, including rashes, ringworm on the scalp, even damage to the hair. When the two groups put their heads together and started brainstorming solutions, they came up with one— shower caps for children who play in the sandbox. (See Strategy 20 for more about conflict resolution.)

Though this particular situation put families and professionals on opposite sides at first, eventually they ended up on the same side, with everybody focusing on what was best for the children. Even when the ending isn't so satisfying, the fact that parents mobilize themselves must be seen in a positive light. When they find energy as a group to push for change, and when an issue comes up that the program faces, that energy can be used again. If the funds are cut and the program is in jeopardy, it's possible that the families will team up with the teachers and advocate to save it.

What can families advocate for? Marion Wright Edelman, founder of the Children's Defense Fund (2003), evaluated the progress made since 1973 in key areas related to the lives of children and pointed out that there is still much to be done. Poverty got the worst grade of the key areas, rating a grade D, because although in 1973 1 out of 6 children lived in poverty, the rate has risen to 1 in 5. In a 2000 UNICEF report, the United States ranked next to last among industrialized nations in child poverty. Its infant mortality rate (another key area) put the United States 28th among industrialized nations (far behind France and Germany). Gun violence was another key area. Although child gun deaths have dropped since 1973, an American child is 12 times more likely to die from gunfire than a child in any other industrialized country. There is much work for child advocates to do to improve the lives of children and their families.

What are some approaches to helping parents along the road to advocacy for all children?

APPROACHES

- Realize that families organizing and advocating can be beneficial even though you may disagree with the target of their advocacy efforts. Keep in mind how effectively that energy can be used when you are all on the same side.
- Help families see the big picture. Advocating for children involves speaking out for giving all children access to high-quality, developmentally and culturally appropriate early childhood experiences in rich, safe environments. For that to happen, those who work with young children must be well trained and well paid. At present that is only a dream; the reality is far from there. But child advocates have made progress and will continue to do so, especially if their numbers continue to grow with the additional numbers of families who are served by ECE programs.
- Encourage advocacy even when the need isn't evident and teach parents how to be effective advocates. Recognize all the places that advocacy works, such as school boards and other governing bodies, regulatory agencies, and lawmakers at the community level, state level, and even the national level. Early childhood education has benefited greatly in the past from family advocacy efforts.
- If families don't organize themselves, help them. Recognize potential leaders among families and nurture their leadership qualities. Start by brushing up on your own leadership skills. Debra Sullivan's book (2003) *Learning to Lead* has many useful ideas.
- Help families understand the many courses of advocacy action. The following are just a few suggestions.
  - Creating or joining an advocacy group
  - Collecting information about a critical issue
  - Finding and sharing research that relates to the issue and formulating a position statement
  - Forming or joining a legislative telephone or e-mail tree
  - Keeping up with the issue in the media and writing letters to the editor
  - Understanding how laws are made
  - Developing a relationship with lawmakers and keeping in touch about the issues that concern children and families

One Person Can Make a Difference

Here is a story about what one town did to respond to child abuse in their community (Gonzalez-Mena, 2006): When a baby died as the result of abuse, a group of residents, led by one individual, decided to do something. This was in the time when child abuse was just beginning to be recognized as widespread and a threat to children's mental and physical health. Though laws were in place at this time, the laws were not enough for this particular group of citizens who wanted to prevent abuse in their community, not just punish it. This motivation on their part coincided with some funding set aside for prevention, intervention, and treatment of child abuse. The group went to work.

First they established a hotline for parents to call, just to talk, when they felt as though they might not be able to control themselves. Then they began to educate the community about child abuse and about using the hotline. This group soon discovered that what parents needed was a variety of support services. Some needed parenting information and skills, some needed relief child care, some needed a job, some needed a place to live, and some just needed relief from the many stresses in their lives that led them to take out their frustrations on their children. The picture was much bigger than anyone had ever suspected.

Today many of these services are in place, including parent support and education groups, relief child care, an emergency aid fund, part-time temporary home service with a helper coming into the home to help with household and child management, and other services. In addition they offer an innovative service they call "phone friend" for children who come home from school to an empty house. All this because one person cared and figured out how to involve others in advocacy.

3

ADVOCACY: PARENTS CONCERNED ABOUT SCHOOL READINESS

RATIONALE

Readiness issues can be a major subject of advocacy as parents enter early childhood programs. A generalization that holds true in most cases is that families want their children to do well in school. Their ideas about what should happen before kindergarten vary greatly. Early childhood educators may also have varied opinions about this subject, but those who have been trained in early childhood principles and practices are likely to have a developmental view, which many parents do not share. Thus, conflicts can arise. It's not unusual for a family or a group of families to push for early academics, for example, hoping that their children will be reading before kindergarten, giving them a head start. When professionals argue the perspective of developmental appropriateness, they may convince some families, but others will dig in harder in order to push their point of view.

Sometimes the family's ideas come from messages they hear based on misinterpretations of brain development research. The pressure for early academics is strong from all sides. The more of that those who have a sophisticated understanding can get to the media and put on public awareness campaigns, then the less work the early childhood professionals will have to discuss misunderstandings with parents.

Sometimes ideas about teaching academics arise from cultural differences rather than misunderstandings about brain research. For example, a Chinese mother's own experience in learning to read in her native language developed because learning characters takes different skills than learning to read in a language that uses an alphabet. She thinks her child should be sitting down memorizing words instead of playing with play dough and finger paint at preschool. Instead of arguing with this mother, it would be good if the child's teacher could listen to what she has to say, even if the teacher doesn't agree with her about what's best for the child at this stage of development. Staying away from arguing creates more of a partnership atmosphere. Instead of arguing, create a dialogue with this mother in the interest of collaboration, even if it is hard to do.

One prerequisite for entering a dialogue is for early childhood education professionals to explore their own attitudes toward particular parents or parents in general. (See Strategy 7.) Also, they should do some soul searching about what they truly believe and explore emotional hotspots that can get in the way of good listening. It is also useful if they can become articulate about the program's policy on readiness so they can explain it to parents who have a different idea without coming on too strong and without arguing. If professionals believe in the policy, they can put aside their defensiveness and learn about a different perspective from their own. Thus, the people in question can create a useful dialogue. Once they have heard each other enough so they have a bigger picture than originally, maybe they can stop taking sides and begin to figure out what is best for this child or a particular group of children in this setting.

This is one of the many situations where good listening skills are necessary. Professionals need to make sure families feel that they are heard. They also need to work hard to understand just what it is that they want. If after some dialoguing there is still disagreement, conflict resolution or consensus building skills are needed. (See Strategy 20.) Be sure that any process toward resolution builds the relationship instead of tearing it down.

Getting children excited about learning is a goal common to most early childhood programs. Sharing that goal with parents can be useful. The joy of learning comes when children are encouraged to become creative, competent explorers and problem solvers. Play and exploration may not look like educational activities to some parents, but when they understand that their children are learning how to learn, they may come to appreciate the approach as useful.

Notice how this setting for play is in a print-rich environment. One aspect of readiness is what is called early literacy, which involves books and beginning letter recognition.

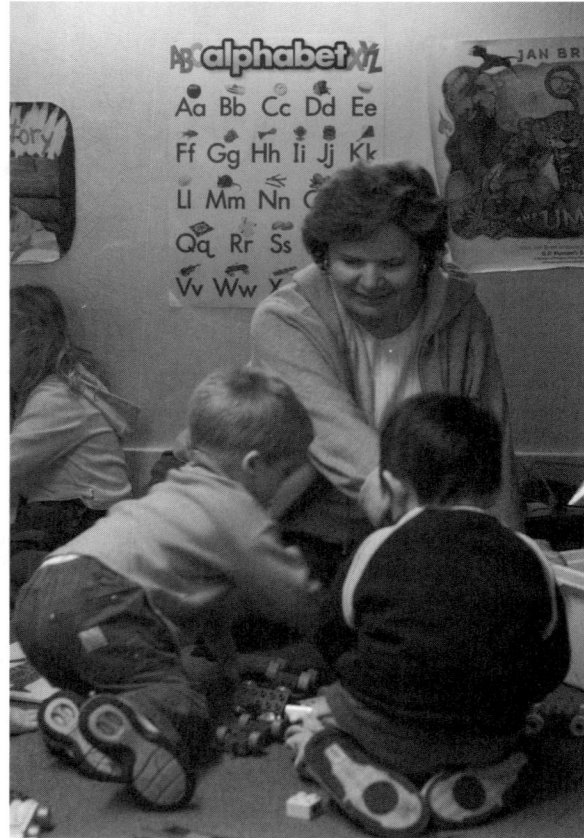

APPROACHES

- Regard a child's exploratory tendencies as an important learning skill. In early childhood, exploration may be more physical than mental, yet those same qualities are what inventors, discoverers, and creators throughout history have used to add to the body of knowledge that exists today. How many explorers go straight to their goal? Not many. Amazing things are discovered while meandering.

- Hone your observation skills and help parents hone theirs so that the value they put on play is increased when they observe what their children are learning as they play. They may even come to see the benefits of allowing free play for longer periods (rather than regarding it as recess—a time to rest from learning). When adults understand how capable most children are of rich creative play, they may interrupt it less and step back so they don't direct or take over.

- Model resourcefulness yourself so children see you as a learner. When children ask why, work with them to find the answer. Further more, let parents know what you are doing and invite them to be part of the process.

- Help parents see how they can use encouragement rather than praise so children are more likely to regard learning as its own reward and depend less on adult recognition of success. Help parents understand the benefits of emphasizing intrinsic rewards that come from the inside by saying, "You must feel so good about what you just accomplished there." Extrinsic rewards are rewards from the outside and make children dependent on somebody else for motivation to learn. Extrinsic rewards can be social rewards—like praise or something tangible like a piece of candy. Use devices such as star charts sparingly.

- Don't argue about any of the preceding suggestions. Become aware of the difference between an argument and a dialogue. The purpose of a dialogue is to understand—not to win. The idea is to expand one's knowledge rather than trying to persuade the other person to accept a different point of view.

- Instead of arguing, offer the families opportunities to observe you with their children and then model what you believe in. The idea is not to win the family over, but rather to expand their views—just as your goal should be to expand your own views through observation of them with their children as well as ongoing dialogue with the family.
- When creating a dialogue, remember that communication involves listening as well as talking. Sometimes we have to listen twice as much as we talk if we are to gain a bigger picture and a deeper understanding.

4 ANTIBIAS ENVIRONMENT

RATIONALE

Although *antibias* is a word that some people find unnecessarily negative, it belongs to a particular tradition that those in early childhood education should know about. The term *pro-diversity* puts a positive spin on the word but doesn't connect it to the antibias movement in the same way. Many early childhood education professionals and parents first heard of the movement in the 1980s from the book, *The Antibias Curriculum*, written by Louise Derman-Sparks (1987) and the Antibias Curriculum Task Force.

What is an antibias environment? Let's start with a typical early childhood environment before the antibias movement began. You could walk into almost any child care center or classroom and look around at what was on the walls, in the dramatic play area (often called "housekeeping corner" then), in the book area, and in the refrigerator. You would find pictures, books, and puzzles representing families and children of European roots. Somewhere you'd find "community helpers" who were White and also segregated by gender. The firefighters and police officers were all men, as were the doctors. The teachers, nurses, and librarians were all women. Although the food may have been that of the area the classroom was in, it was food with which European Americans in that region were most familiar. Even if the staff was diverse, the environment didn't reflect this diversity or their backgrounds. Furthermore, it was obvious that the people in charge were from one group and the aides and cleaning people were from another. This isn't ancient history. You can still find this kind of situation in some programs today, although there has been some change.

Now let's take a walk through an antibias environment. Pretend that you enter the door of a classroom or child care center. You look around and see pictures on the wall representing the diversity of the children and their families—also of the greater society. You notice that some pictures are of women in a variety of jobs and roles, as well as various pictures of men. When you walk over to the book area, you see that same diversity is represented not only in the pictures and stories but in the languages also. Books are available in the various home languages of the children. Some are commercial and some are homemade. In the dramatic play area, which is set up for housekeeping play today, you see objects and containers of food products found in the homes of the families in the programs. A mother is sitting at one of the tables, helping several children make tortillas for a snack. At circle time this week, a grandfather came in to tell the children a story from his culture to the whole group. Today's circle time is made up of a small group of children sitting on the floor with a teacher who is speaking a language other than English. She is using two persona dolls to tell a story. These are dolls the children are familiar with—they already know their names, personalities, and family histories and something about their cultures. The story is about something that happened between these two dolls. The story is familiar to the children, because something similar happened recently in the play yard between some of the children. The teacher asks the children to help the two dolls resolve their problem. The children contribute lots of ideas.

Creative teachers have always found ways to bring diversity into the classroom; one way is by using parents as resources. The supply catalogs once offered only a few items representing diversity. Now, of course, you can buy "people" crayons in many skin tones—whereas there used to be one "flesh-colored" crayon in a box and it was pale. Community helpers are also diversified.

It isn't just "stuff" that makes an environment an antibias one. An antibias environment is also affected by the attitudes and behaviors of the people in it. Organizational matters affect the environment too. An organization with the goal of an antibias environment has a variety of people in all

Part of an antibias approach is creating an environment that welcomes men as much as it welcomes women.

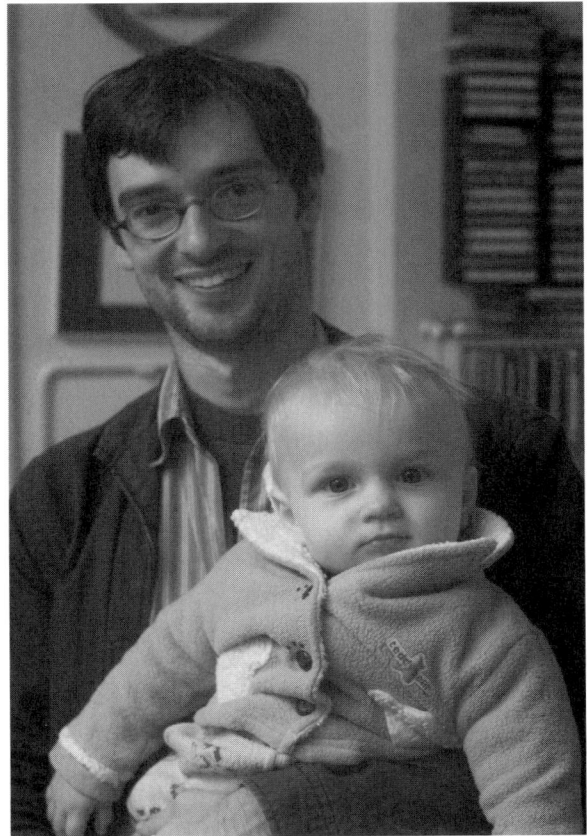

levels of positions and job roles—the boss isn't necessarily a European American person and the cleaning person and gardener aren't new immigrants. Antibias also shows up in the way people communicate with each other, as well as the attitudes of respect and openness that are displayed.

APPROACHES

- Analyze the environment you are in and see if it welcomes all people who use it.
- Does it reflect people who don't come into it, but who are in the community?
- Consider how to make any environment welcoming and reflective of all people.
- Become aware of your own behaviors that show your biases and prejudices.
- Respect all families and don't make snap judgments about them.
- Keep a positive attitude in the face of differences.
- Give families credit for having funds of knowledge that may be quite different from your own.
- Learn about their funds of knowledge.
- Involve families—ask them to bring in aspects of their culture.
- Pay attention to what goes on between families in the program and consider helping them sort out differences like you help children. But remember, you can't be all things to all people, so if the role of facilitator of adults doesn't come easily, maybe somebody else should do it.

This classroom is in a rural school on the West Coast that has a number of Spanish-speaking families, mostly from Mexico.

SUNNY VALLEY SCHOOL NEWS

SPECIAL EVENTS

Jason Lopez reports on the Cinco de Mayo Celebration.

On May 5th we celebrated Cinco de Mayo. We had three performances, one by Mrs. Gomez's class, one by Ms. Johnson's class and one by Mr. Smith's class. Mrs. Gomez's class did a song called Rancho Grande. Ms. Johnson's class did a dance. Mr. Smith's class did a play. We learned that Cinco de Mayo is all about how the Mexicans won an important battle. At the assembly, Jerrick Palacov, our student council president gave each classroom their own flower.

Jason Lopez

Taking an antibias approach means recognizing the cultures in the class.

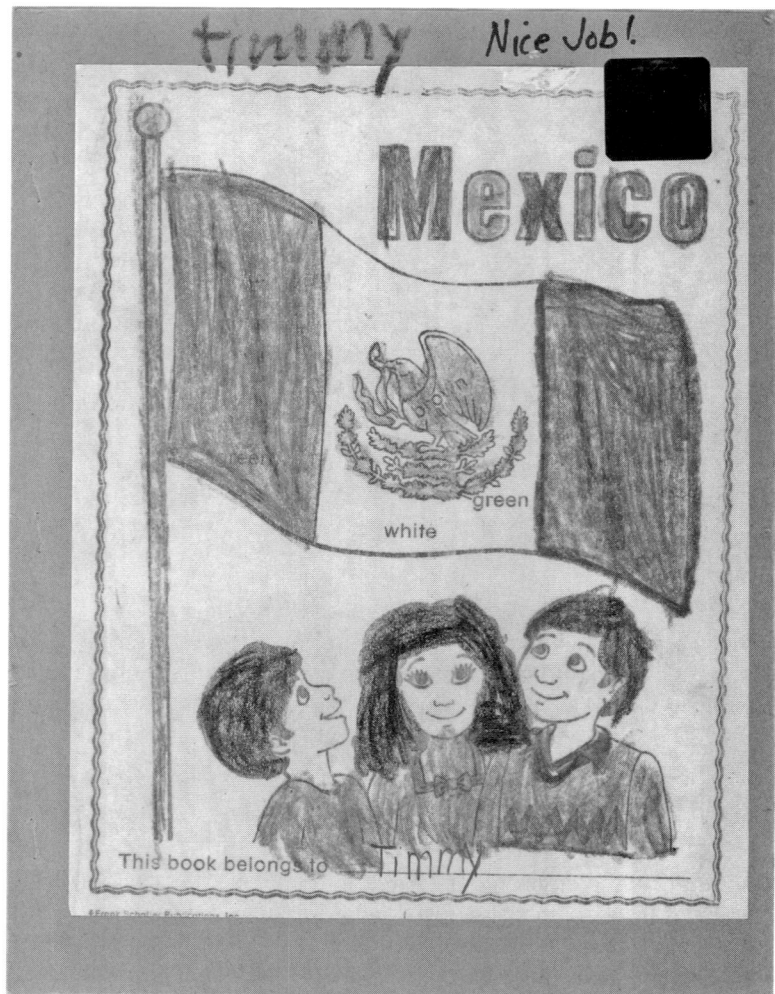

5 ASSESSMENT

RATIONALE

Every early childhood and early care and education program is involved in assessment of the children's progress whether or not they have a formal assessment process and reporting procedure. Some assess informally through observation and recordkeeping. Others have various kinds of tests, some focused on academics, others on developmental norms. Others use charts and developmental profiles. Some programs use parents in the assessment process by having them fill out forms and keeping up through ongoing conversations. Some programs are much more concerned about assessments than others; some of these have regulations dictating assessment or funding bodies that require them.

An important issue to recognize with assessment is that in any kind of formal or even informal testing situation, who does the testing matters. The younger the child, the greater the chance that stranger anxiety will interfere. Imagine a toddler taken out of the classroom with peers and a familiar teacher and placed in a new room with a stranger and asked to perform certain tasks. Stranger anxiety can make a huge difference in test scores. Expectations of the tester as well as the person being tested also matter.

At the Pikler Institute, a residential nursery in Budapest, Hungary, assessment is ongoing and based on observation by people who have a relationship with the children. The staff at this institute never sets up a testing situation or asks a child to perform some task. All of the assessment is done in the children's natural, everyday environment.

It's hard to make generalizations about assessment procedures or about parents' involvement in and attitudes about assessment. Some parents are very concerned about their children's progress and others are less concerned. Some parents compare their children to other children; they want some kind of grading system or developmental charts to figure out where their children stand. Other parents feel strongly that their children are individuals and it is a disservice to compare one to the other or to a group or norm. Families who have children with special needs may have a very different view about assessment based on their child's strengths and needs. They may arrive in a program with a whole history of assessment procedures. (See Strategy 44, Talking with Families When Concerns Arise, for more information about this subject.)

So considering all the different ways of assessing, the different mandates, and the parental attitudes towards assessment, what are some strategies for working with parents around assessment issues?

APPROACHES

- Always communicate about the children's strengths to parents. Focus on the strengths instead of on the deficits. Don't lie, but don't be so taken by negatives that you can't see the positives.
- Make sure the assessment process—formal or informal—is broad enough to include all of the child's strengths.
- Involve families in assessment procedures to make sure that the process is linguistically and culturally appropriate. For example, assessments that involve language must be done in the child's strongest language, whether English or some other language. The rationale for nondiscriminatory and culturally appropriate assessment and involving parents comes from the 1997 Individual with

Disabilities Education Improvement Act (IDEA) and from the National Association for the Education of Young Children (NAEYC).

- When assessing, focus on process rather than on product alone.
- Use a portfolio approach in order to document assessments. That way you can give families examples of what you're basing your assessment on. If the child is especially creative with block building, take photos and videos of the process and the product for the portfolio.
- When discussing the results of assessment, recognize that parents and other family members bring their own memories and experiences about school to any discussion that involves assessment of their child, whether at a parent-teacher conference or in casual conversation when parent and teacher happen to meet. Those memories may bring uncomfortable feelings. (See more about this subject in Strategy 18, Conferences.)
- Most parents have great hopes for their children and it's your job to keep those hopes intact. Using the words *pass* and *fail*, for example, when giving an infant a development test may have a negative impact on parents and dash their hopes and dreams. IQ scores may have an even worse effect. It's wrong to make parents see strong limits to their children's potential based on an assessment process.

Here is story about assessment: In an early intervention program center for infants and toddlers with identified developmental delays, disabilities, and those at risk for them, a chart of developmental milestones was hanging over the diapering counter. Every time a mother put her baby on that counter to change diapers, that chart stared back at her. One time in a parent meeting, one mother expressed her feelings about the chart and every member of the group shared her distress at seeing that chart when their babies didn't match it. They had a hard time not comparing, especially when the comparisons were so available. Upon hearing the feelings expressed, the staff took down the chart.

Assessment can be done in the child's natural environment through observation. Notice how close the teacher is standing, just in case this boy needs her. Once he gets good at climbing, she won't need to be so close. This scene shows an example of a teacher using informal assessment so she can respond appropriately to the child's needs.

This report card for a first grader shows a method of assessment. Notice that the comments focus on the child's strengths.

This progress report goes home with every family on Friday. It is returned on Monday with a signature. The parents get teacher feedback this way and in the form of written notes. The notes are usually answered, so the teacher gets feedback too.

_____'s Weekly Progress Report Date_____

1. Completed   all   some   little   classwork.
2. Completed   all   some   little   homework.
3. Followed classroom rules
        all the time   some of the time   rarely
4. Followed playground/ school rules
        all the time   some of the time   rarely
5. Used friendship and cooperation
        all the time   some of the time   rarely
   Overall,
   I had a great week   okay week   "bumpy" week
Please sign and return on Monday.
I have discussed this report with my child.
Signed _____

6 ATTACHMENT

RATIONALE

Attachment is important for all children. The younger the child, the more attachment comes into the picture in early care and education programs. In infant-toddler programs, creating a relationship with one or a small number of special people is vital. Even if infants and toddlers have a firm and close attachment at home, they still need a relationship that is personal, steady, and ongoing if they spend more than a few hours each time away from the family. Feelings of trust and a sense of security come from attachment.

Research being done on the human brain points to the importance of attachment and caring relationships, especially in the first years of life. Bruce Perry (2006) talks in his lectures and writings about the chemicals that wash over the brain and cause damage when babies experience continual abuse and neglect or live in unusually stressful environments. Without attachment, babies suffer. With a firm, healthy attachment the baby has a better chance of getting through the hard times with less damage (Perry, 2006). The Pikler Institute, a residential nursery for infants and toddlers in Budapest, Hungary, is based on the concept that attachment to caregivers is a vital ingredient of the first years of life and allows even institutionalized babies to grow up to be whole, healthy, and fully functioning adults. (David and Appell, 2001; Gonzalez-Mena, 2004; Petrie and Owen, 2005) Shonkoff and Phillips (2000) have made a strong case for caring relationships. When babies feel secure in a healthy attachment, their brains are able to develop without harmful chemicals interfering. Studies of resilient children indicate that even just one close and caring relationship can make a difference even in the face of continual hardship (Werner, 1995).

Attachment to a caregiver, a teacher, or a provider is a concern for many families. "Will my baby still love me if he spends all that time away from me while I'm working" is an agonizing question many parents ask themselves or their caregivers. The caregiver's response should always be reassuring.

Another related issue arises when families watch their children get attached to someone outside the family. For some it is a relief that their child feels comfortable and safe away from home, but mixed with that can come feelings of being replaced. Some families feel competition for the child's affection. When caregivers and teachers seem to know more, have better skills, and can handle their children better than the family can, the feelings of competition can be devastating.

Lilian Katz (1977) reminds us that being a teacher, caregiver, or provider is very different from being a parent, though children should be attached to both. The following are some of the differences:

- The child's attachment to the family is and should be closer than the attachment to the professionals.
- The child has a history with the family and a future. The relationship of the ECE professional is more short term, with the exception of some family child care providers who may work with the same child for 11 or 12 years and with the family even longer if there are siblings. But even then, the future of the child is still in the hands of the family, not in those of the professional.
- The length of the relationship of child to the ECE professional is less predictable. Children can leave the program at any time if the family changes programs or moves away from the school.

As children grow older, if they have a firm sense of themselves and feel secure in their attachments at home, most don't need such a close one-on-one relationship with an adult in out-of-home programs. Kindergarten and primary teachers have a larger group size and ratio of children to adults, so the amount of one-on-one personal attention drops, as compared to prekindergarten and infant-toddler programs. Skilled teachers who understand the value can still form healthy attachments so that all children feel valued and close to their teacher.

APPROACHES

- Take attachment seriously. If policies to promote attachment aren't already in place, do what you can to create them. Such policies should include:
  - ○ Small group size—the younger the children, the smaller the group needs to be. Starting with infants, a good group size is six infants with two caregivers. This way the caregivers can get to know a reasonable number of children, as well as their families (Lally, 1995). As children get older, the group size can increase. In some states 20 is considered a reasonable group size for kindergarten through third grade.
  - ○ Primary caregivers—especially for children under age 3, each professional should have several children for whom he or she is primarily responsible and works to become attached to. This is not an exclusive relationship, and there should be other caregivers who also know the children individually and as a group (Lally, 1995). By kindergarten, especially if children have learned to be functioning members of a peer group, one teacher will work, though it is desirable to have several adults in the classroom, including some parent volunteers. That way children get more individualized attention from adults. Family participation is another benefit.
  - ○ Continuity of care—instead of "promoting" young children to a new room and teacher as they reach a new stage of development or have a birthday, keep them together as a group with the same teacher. That means that as infants and toddlers outgrow the environment, the environment either needs to change or the group and teachers need to move together to a new room.

Attachment is important for all children. The younger the child, the more attachment comes into the picture in early care and education programs.

For infants and toddlers, 2 or 3 years gives them and their parents a chance to become attached to the professionals. This approach is called looping in preschool and kindergarten through third grade.

- Communicate with the family about the policies and their purpose. Explain clearly that the attachment to the early childhood professional is not meant to compete with the attachment to the family. The family attachment should always be closer because it is far more important and long-lasting than any other attachment.
- Support the child's attachment to family and acknowledge the child's feelings for the family members to whom he is most attached. Assure parents that they are number one in the child's life.
- Be aware that some families may feel threatened by seeing evidence that their children care about their teachers and do what you can to help them feel more secure. Watch out for the following pitfalls:
  - ○ Encouraging lots of physical affection from children, especially if you see the parent looking uncomfortable when the child comes back for yet another hug and kiss.
  - ○ Letting a child call you mommy or daddy, if such a thing happens. Correct them if they do. Let parents help you decide by what name you should be called.
  - ○ Taking pride in being the first to see a child reach a milestone. "Your baby took his first step today" can be a devastating announcement to a parent who wished they could be there to see it. It doesn't hurt to let the parent make the discovery that the baby is starting to walk and announce it to you.
- Look inside yourself and explore your own feelings about a particular child or family. It's natural for professionals to have strong feelings about a child or group of children. Some professionals go through a "savior stage" of wanting to rescue children from their parents. Acknowledge your feelings and at the same time become fully aware of your actions. You can accept the feelings without *acting on* them.
- Understand that professionals establishing attachment should focus on optimal distance, while promoting optimal closeness in family attachment.

7

ATTITUDES OF PROFESSIONALS: EXAMINING AND ADJUSTING ONE'S OWN

RATIONALE

Some of the biggest barriers to communicating and working effectively with families are the attitudes of many early childhood professionals toward families and families' attitudes toward them. Some early childhood education professionals have a bias against parents—setting themselves above the group with whom they are supposed to work. This may be an unconscious attitude, but it comes out in behaviors. It also shows up in language when professionals generalize. Conscious or unconscious stereotypes also get in the way of forming partnerships with parents. For example, the following has been heard in staff meetings more than once—"Oh, you know how parents are," said with a sigh. That's a generalization. "Oh *those* parents" said critically can indicate a stereotypical idea that parents of a certain group don't really care about their children.

Looking into the reasons behind a negative attitude toward families, we can see a pattern that has come down through the ages. When one group feels downtrodden, lacks self-esteem, and is devalued by society, members of that group sometimes look around to see who they can regard as lower than themselves. Because of the humble beginnings of early care and education as a field, practitioners have not garnered the esteem (such as it is) of teachers in other levels of education. Furthermore, early childhood education has not been highly regarded by the public, who often equate it with babysitting. One U.S. president suggested that child care could be replaced by volunteers, grandmothers, and other kindly community women so that the taxes that go into public-supported child care could be saved. One huge argument against such a step is that care and education can never be separated. (See Strategy 11 for further discussion of this issue.) Another is that training makes a difference in quality. Though early childhood education professionals have nothing to be ashamed of, many still have difficulty feeling good about themselves, especially when the pay of the average early childhood education professional keeps them at the poverty level on the economic scale.

While professionals are trying to establish their professionalism, they may stress their funds of knowledge and ignore those of the family. They may also take on airs they consider to be professional—such as remaining cool, distant, and emotionally detached. ECE as a profession is still exploring what it means to be professional and retain their status while building relationships with each other and with the families and children they serve. Being too emotional and closely attached becomes a problem, but remaining distant, removed, and detached is also a problem.

The other side of the picture is how some family members treat early childhood education professionals. One explanation may be that some family members find themselves much higher on the socioeconomic ladder and look down on their early childhood education staff or provider. They are used to having power at work and may see the people who serve their children as underlings. One infant-toddler caregiver, when told she had to wear an apron, said she would refuse to do so because she in no way wanted to suggest to the parents that she was like their maid.

Another explanation for negative parent attitudes toward teachers and care and education providers may be that the family perceives that they are in the same boat and have the same low status. Family members may seek to rise above that level so they can look down on the ECE staff or provider.

Whoever designed this space for parents had a good attitude toward them. Often there is no reception area in early care and education centers. This one has comfortable seating for the whole family—a real bonus!

APPROACHES

- Become aware of when you are generalizing and catch yourself. When one parent is making things difficult, it's not uncommon for the ECE professional to complain to a colleague about parents in general. Remember, just because one parent is difficult doesn't mean that all parents are the same.
- Avoid stereotyping. Just by living in a racist and sexist society, we unconsciously take in stereotypes. The media is full of them—for example, making fun of people with accents or of people with differing abilities. Become aware of your own stereotypes and move beyond them. Making an effort to know individuals from a group that you have a tendency to stereotype will broaden your view of them.
- When someone bothers you, do some self-reflection. Often the traits in people we don't like are the same traits that we have in ourselves but don't see. They may not show because we are so busy suppressing them, but when they appear in others, it touches us deeply where we are most vulnerable. This is called projection and shows up in the saying that we are more like our worst enemies than our friends.
- Be aware of how powerful roles are. The teacher who is also a parent can forget that when relating to parents in his or her program.
- Work on your own self-esteem. Take care of yourself. Stand up for yourself. Learn self-assertion skills.
- Work on your professionalism. As a member of the early childhood education profession, you are part of something bigger than you are.
- Recognize that the body of knowledge you have or are gaining is important. Even though you want to be open and sensitive to parents who don't know what you know doesn't mean that you should discount your own knowledge.

Here's a story about how strong the roles we play can be and how they influence our behavior: An early childhood educator who was also a parent went to her daughter's school for a parent-teacher conference. Though she was friends with her daughter's teacher and had talked to him a number of times, once she got into classroom, she began to feel different. She wasn't there as a friend; she was there as a parent. When she sat on the little chair on the other side of the table, she felt a little intimidated, though she was aware that it was partly the furniture influencing her. When the teacher got out his grade book, her daughter's folder, and his notes, she felt stiff and uncomfortable. He seemed to feel the same. Again she was aware that the roles they were both playing were influencing their interactions. Once the conference was over and the teacher offered her a cookie, the tone of the meeting changed. When she got up to walk out, she was herself again. She was conscious of what was happening while it was happening, but couldn't seem to lighten up the situation.

8 AUTHORITY: ADULT BEHAVIORS RELATED TO

RATIONALE

A second issue related to authority arises when the behaviors of the adult in charge don't mirror the kinds of behaviors the child is used to. Images of authority are important when it comes to child guidance. For example, one prekindergarten teacher learned in her courses and field work how to guide behavior by using gentle words and a neutral tone of voice. Some children ignore this teacher. These children are beginning to be perceived as having problem behavior, yet the real problem is that the children don't think the teacher means what she says because of her soft approach. These children are used to the way the adults in their families and extended kinship networks assert their authority at home and in the neighborhood, including stern voices, meaningful facial expressions, and strong body language, which are followed by immediate action if the words and "the look" don't work. For example, Lonnie Snowden (1984; Gonzalez-Mena, 2005) says, "The Black community invests effective responsibility for control of children's behavior in an extensive network of adults. . . . Because of this extended parenting, children's behavior receives proper monitoring and more immediate sanctions than is the norm in American society. Children may be expected to develop more active exploratory tendencies and assertive styles, since respected external agencies can be counted on to reliably check excess."

When authority figures behave in ways that aren't familiar to the children, they can feel confused (Phillips, 1995). Furthermore, some children are used to firm, strict, and sometimes physical guidance, and without it they keep testing the limits. They may even come to the conclusion that the teacher doesn't care what they do. These children can end up labeled as problem children (Hale-Benson, 1986).

It's important to note that firm limits actually give some children more freedom because they know somebody will stop them if they go too far. When the teacher just talks and doesn't stop them, they continue to push to find out what the limits are. They don't recognize that they are getting guidance and direction from the adults in that situation, but those adults aren't like the ones at home. Instead of being strict and insisting on certain behaviors, they are stressing individual choice. The lessons then come from the children living with the consequences of their actions. They don't scold or threaten. They don't punish. They allow natural consequences within reason— ones that don't harm the child but may feel uncomfortable. When there are no natural consequences, they set up the situation so there are logical consequences (Dreikurs, 1990). The adult can do this without even changing facial expression or tone of voice. This can all be done in a matter-of-fact manner.

Cynthia Ballenger (1992) writes about the problem of children's confusion over adults' authority when Haitian children encounter teachers who stress individual choice and living with the consequences of the choice. The Haitian teachers didn't think in terms of individual choice but defined behavior as good and bad. They warned children that bad behavior brings shame on the family. They told the children that they had a responsibility to be good and scolded them when they weren't good. The teachers regarded reprimands as ways to strengthen the relationship and show children that someone cares about them and their behavior. That is a contrast to more neutral approaches that avoid reprimands, allow children to make choices to discover what the consequences are, and put responsibility on the individual.

So how do you work with parents around differences in how children are expected to relate to authority?

APPROACHES

- When the teacher acts one way and the family another, this situation calls for some serious discussion. If you already have a relationship with the parent and there is mutual trust, it will be easier to talk about how to help the child get along both at school and at home.
- Start by observing the parent with the child and suspend judgment if the parent's behavior doesn't match what you think is the right approach to guidance.
- Have the parent observe how you handle misbehavior and talk about it afterwards.
- If there is a drastic difference, expect the dilemma to be resolved eventually, but probably not right away. Try to learn about the parent's approach, what the reasons behind it are, and what the expected outcomes are. If this is a cross-cultural situation, you may both have something to learn about the other person's cultural differences.
- Explain your approach and why you do what you do, but don't try to sell it to the parent. This should be a mutual exchange of information.
- Continue to work on the relationship.
- Try different approaches with the child if the ones you use don't work and the ones the parents use do. That doesn't mean you have to give up your values or imitate the parent. By all means, don't do anything you perceive as harmful to the child.
- Open your mind to the idea that what you see as harmful may not be in the context of the family or culture. For example, if you are trained in early childhood education principles, you won't use name calling as a way to guide behavior because, in general, such a practice is regarded as detrimental to children's self-image. If parents call children a name or use some kind of label, you can't judge what that name or label means to the child, especially if it is a cross-cultural situation and in a language you don't speak.

9

AUTHORITY: TEACHER OR
PARENT—WHO HAS IT WHEN?

RATIONALE

One issue that sometimes comes up between early childhood education professionals and families is who is the authority in what situation. In school when a parent is there and his child breaks a rule, should the parent step back and let the teacher handle it or take care of it himself? In a family child care home, a child starts jumping on the couch; is it the parent's place to stop him (even if jumping on the couch is allowed at their home) or the provider's job? Another example occurs at a child care center when the staff and parents put on a party for newcomers to get acquainted. The children are invited. When a group of them gets too wild, whose job is it to settle them down?

Sometimes this is not a problem. It may be that one party or the other steps forward and manages the behavior and both are in agreement about what is the right thing to do. But at other times both parties wait for the other to do something, resulting in out-of-bounds behavior of the child, lack of guidance, and even damaged property. Or such situations can result in a sense of confusion or insecurity on the part of the child who knows she is out of bounds and expects someone to do something about it. Alternatively, if one adult steps back and the other steps in because the other isn't doing anything, that action may result in hurt feelings or resentment on the part of one or both adults.

APPROACHES

- Determine who will be the authority in each case. Who has the primary responsibility for the child's behavior in each setting or situation when both parent and professional are present at the same time? This is not something you can look up in a book—it has to be decided among the parties involved.
- Plan ahead, as in the previous story.
- When a situation occurs where the authority issues haven't been settled, discuss the situation out in the open.
- Anticipate situations and discuss them ahead of time. For example, one preschool center discussed at a parent meeting the expectations they had for parents to be in charge of their own children at an upcoming party with family members and staff. The families agreed that it would be up to them, even though the party was taking place in the center where the teachers usually provided guidance for the children.

Another issue around authority relates to who has what information. The photo on page 46 shows an example of a first-grade teacher discussing a child's progress with his father. In this case, the teacher knows what goes on at school and how the child performs. She not only has her observations and interactions to give her information but also has actual records and samples of the child's work. Just because she has information about the child at school doesn't mean that she ignores what the father knows about the child outside of school. His information is important to her, just as her information is important to the father. Notice that the child is part of the conference. This discussion isn't going on behind his back, but includes his viewpoint, information, and experience as well.

Parents may not have all the information about child development, curriculum, and how to teach groups of children that teachers have, but they have plenty of information that the teacher doesn't have about their own child, his history, his interests, and their plans for his future. They are the authority on how their family works, on being members of their culture. Each has other areas of expertise as well that vary by family and by individual. The following are some strategies for thinking about, respecting, and responding to the authority that lies in the family:

- Respect each family's authority over its own children.
- Get to know family members, and you will discover their many areas of expertise. Some of these people can be resources for your classroom or center.
- Appreciate the funds of knowledge that families have and focus on their strengths. (See Strategy 43, Strengths.)
- Find ways to share what the families know and what you know. Everybody will be richer.

10 BEHAVIOR CHANGES: TALKING WITH PARENTS ABOUT

RATIONALE

Todd is having a hard time lately in the center. He used to be easygoing and able to get along with everybody, but lately he has changed a good deal. He refuses to comply with the rules. He argues with everybody, including the teachers. He always seems tired, and sometimes he just sits and stares off into space. He has always been a happy, active child. The way he is acting now has his teacher worried. At a staff meeting, the teachers discuss Todd's change in behavior. Is this a stage he is going through? "I think something must be going on at home," said one of the teachers. "I'm going to talk to his mother, and I'll let you know what she says."

Talking to his mother is a fine idea, but if the purpose of the conversation is to ask about what is going on at home that would explain the change in his behavior, the teacher should reconsider. This approach to understanding child behavior is so common in early care and education that most professionals don't think twice about it.

Jim Greenman (2003) is an advocate for not prying into a family's private life in the name of understanding the child better. He says, "Respect for parents demands that, unless the situation is one of abuse or neglect, the parents control what information they wish to share" (p. 317). Greenman questions that teachers have any more right to know about what goes on in the family than the family has a right to know about the teachers' private lives. If a teacher is going through a divorce, should a notice go home to the parents to watch for changes in the behavior of the children because their teacher is so stressed out? What if the parents were told to be understanding with their children and give them extra attention because of what is going on at school?

If you can see that a child is under stress, do you really need to know why? Will you treat him differently if you know the roots of his stress? Why not just support him and give him what he needs regardless of what is going on at home? Greenman suggests giving the child under stress flexibility, warmth, and nurturing. If he wants to talk about how he feels, the teacher can listen. If the parents come to her and want to share what's going on, that's very different from the teacher asking and then reporting to the other teachers. That's unprofessional unless the teacher has permission to share the information.

The following are some ideas about how to relate to parents when you see a change of behavior in their children.

APPROACHES

- Be a good observer. Be clear about what the changes are and under what circumstances they occur.
- Respond to the child's behavior in ways that help him relax, if possible. Let him know he has your support and understanding. Do what you can to meet his needs.
- If you see that he's feeling pressure while in the classroom, do what you can to ease the pressure.
- Set and keep limits for the child, but do so in calm and gentle ways. See if you can make things easier for the child at school. Meet his needs as best you can. If you determine that he is feeling pressure in the classroom, ease off.
- If you ask the parent to talk with you about the situation at school, be prepared to share your observations and what you are doing to respond. Report what has worked and what hasn't. Listen to any suggestions the parent might have about how to work with the behaviors.

- Make sure your observations are reported in nonjudgmental terms. Describe behavior without putting value judgments on it.
- Respect the parent's right to privacy. Don't ask what is going on at home. If the parent wants to share with you what is happening, keep this information confidential. Offer your support and use your best listening skills. Don't offer advice.
- If the parent hasn't already given you suggestions for how to work with her child in school, ask her and then listen to her ideas. Give them a try. They just might make a difference.
- You can do all of the above without needing to know if the parents are getting a divorce, if the father got laid off or is in jail, if there's a new baby in the family (although the parents or the child are likely to voluntarily share that news with you), or whether grandma just died and grandpa came to live with them. Any one of those situations could cause a change in behavior. You can work with the change without knowing the reason it came about.

11   CARE AND EDUCATION: THE LINK

RATIONALE

The title of Jim Greenman's book *Caring Spaces, Learning Places: Children's Environments That Work* (2005) makes two points, even if you never read the book. Care and education are linked, and the environment is an important factor in both caring and learning. Loris Malaguzzi made a related point when he said that the environment is a teacher. Words relate to concepts. Consider the initials ECE. Some people say those letters stand for early childhood education. Indeed, a number of years ago those in the field all would have said the initials stood for early childhood education. In those years, let's say, back in the 1960s when Head Start was born, programs for young children were separated into categories—two major ones were educational programs and child care programs. When ECE expanded into kindergarten and the primary grades, it then included children under age 8. Programs for those children were also split between educational ones and child care ones. Children went to school to be educated and then to child care to be watched over before and after school and on school vacations.

This book uses the initials ECE to mean early care and education to emphasize that you can't separate care from education. Children aren't cars—they can't be parked in the morning and picked up in the afternoon and expected to be exactly how you left them except for a new layer of dust. Children are always learning, whether they are in a designated educational program or not. It's important to recognize that fact because otherwise their learning is haphazard and may be detrimental to their own well-being and that of others. Once everyone acknowledges that children learn while being cared for and must be cared for while they are learning, programs for those children can be improved.

It may be easier to see the link between care and education in programs for infants and toddlers. Their physical care takes up much of the time. However, care and education are not necessarily linked in the minds of many, even for infants and toddlers. Back in the 1960s and 1970s infant care programs were unusual, and most children under age 3 were in informal settings with relatives or in family child care; then educational programs for infants came into being. Based on research that led to infant stimulation, two groups of people began to be interested in infant stimulation: special education experts and parents who wanted "better babies"—those who wanted their babies to reach milestones faster and prove they were smarter than the average baby. Today, the latest brain research is sometimes misread by those who still separate education from care.

Two historic and notable exceptions to the trend to stimulate in the name of education are Magda Gerber, an infant specialist, and Emmi Pikler, a pediatrician, both Hungarians who have had influence on the field of infant-toddler care. They both agreed that education and care can never be separated. Education comes out of the relationship that is developed between infants and their caregivers during the essential activities of daily living, called caregiving routines. When diapering, feeding, grooming, dressing, and other such activities are done in a human-to-human way rather than mindlessly, attachment grows and from that attachment comes education. Children learn language, for one thing. They also learn about how their bodies work and how to cooperate with their caregivers. When they receive close adult attention during those kinds of activities and during the rest of the time are given freedom to move and learn in a safe, rich environment in which other children are present, they become competent learners—a major goal of any educational approach. Care and education together make the difference.

What may not be so obvious is that caring is important for children of preschool age—those who are 3 to 5 years of age. What about when the children get into school and the physical care part is their own responsibility and takes place mostly during recess and lunchtime when the ratios of children to adults greatly increases? Caring extends beyond just physical care and is still linked. Nell Noddings (1992) is a major spokesperson for the idea that care and education are always linked—no matter the age of the child or student. She focuses on caring not as an attribute or quality (an individual virtue) but as an encounter (an interaction). She writes about a caring relationship, which she says is "in its most basic form a connection or encounter between two human beings—a carer and a recipient of care or cared-for" (p. 15). She sees caring as a two-way connection or encounter because each party feels something toward the other. In other words, no matter how much one party cares, if the other doesn't, then it's not a caring relationship. Caring is a state of consciousness characterized by engrossment, which Nodding defines as an open, nonselective receptivity to the cared-for. It's a type of attention.

Simon Weil (1951, p. 115 in Noddings, p. 16) wrote about a kind of consciousness that describes engrossment. "This way of looking is first of all attentive. The soul empties itself of all its own contents in order to receive into itself the being it is looking at, just as he is, in all his truth. Only he who is capable of attention can do this." Motivational displacement, that is, motivational energy, is flowing toward others and their project. We move our fingers in sympathetic reaction to a child struggling with shoe laces. We want to respond in a way that furthers the other's purpose or project. The cared-for receives the caring and shows that it has been received, and the recognition (reward) becomes part of the carer's engrossment. We don't have to always keep the same roles; mature relationships are characterized by mutuality. Strings of encounters result in which parties change places.

Nodding makes scholarly arguments as she lays out her philosophy in her books—one of which is *The Challenge to Care in Schools*. She questions the idea of competition as a major push in educational approaches and says that the school instead should be an environment of caring so that the strengths of all learners can be nurtured. The idea of promoting only academic achievement—specifically language, math, and science—leaves out many learners and contributes to an elitist educational system that educates and rewards some but leaves out many others. She gives many different examples of how people learn and explores how schools can do a better job of approaching the teaching-learning process. She

Here it is easy to see the link between care and education. The child is comfortably seated on a caring adult's lap, while becoming familiar with books. From a number of experiences like this one, he is likely to connect pleasure with reading later in school and throughout his life.

suggests organizing the curriculum around themes of care, which should include caring for the self, for those close to the learner, for others, for animals, for plants, for the earth, for objects, and for ideas. She criticizes what she calls a "shallow educational response to deep social change."

So what does all of this have to do with working with families? Parents are influenced by their own experiences growing up. If competition worked in their favor, they may see competition as something they want their children to participate in, even if it isn't effective in their children's care and education setting. When parents come to understand the ideas related to linking care and education, they may begin to see their own early experiences in a different light. They may be able to better evaluate their children's early experiences. They may even become advocates for all children. (See Strategies 1 and 2, Advocacy.)

Parents are targets for marketers who want to sell them goods and services. Virtually all parents want the best for their children. They want their children to be smart, competent, and successful, and marketers prey on parent's hopes and dreams.

APPROACHES

- Many parents' earliest memories in education are of school, so they use those memories as a model for what they think should happen in their children's early care and education programs. That means they may have misconceptions about what does happen and why. Their ideas about

When care and education are linked, caring comes out in all kinds of ways. Children in this classroom spent a lot of time making Mother's Day cards and at the same time worked on their writing skills.

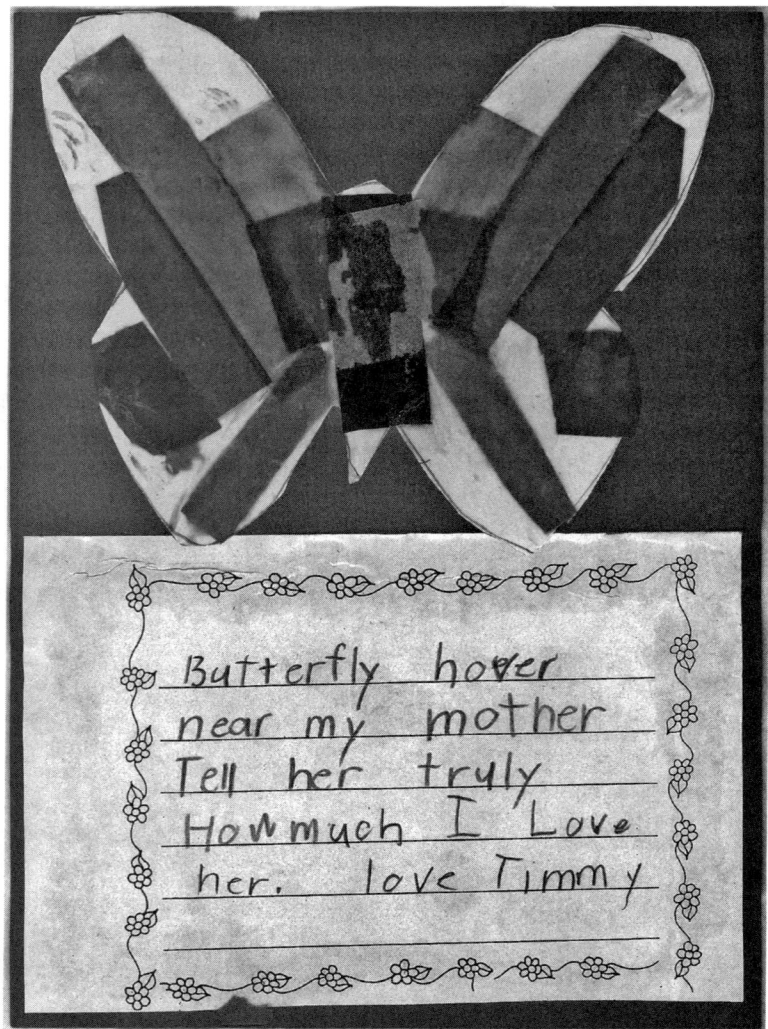

quality early care and education approaches may be very different from reality and from what the research indicates. All this points toward finding ways to give parents the information they need to understand why teachers do what they do. Families can make better decisions about what they want for their children when they are well informed.

- There is an advocacy aspect to helping parents see what quality care and education looks like and understand why it is important. Parents can be strong advocates once they have the knowledge they may be missing. They can in turn educate others about the importance of linking care and education—not seeing them as two separate and distinct approaches to programming.

- As parents begin to understand the role that care plays in education, they may begin to advocate for improved quality in their child's program and in early care and education programs in general.

- When parents see the importance of relationships, it may help them feel less threatened when their children begin to get close to the teacher or caregiver.

- The parents may be willing to talk more about their perception of the links between what happens at home and what happens in the ECE program.

12

CARE AND EDUCATION PRACTICES: WHEN CONFLICTS ARISE

RATIONALE

Dealing with conflicts around care and education practices is a huge subject and weaves itself throughout many of the strategies in this text. Because it is impossible in a small space or even in a lifetime to condense all differences that can occur, this particular strategy focuses on a set of contrasting patterns that influences how people see children, determine what they need, and develop care and education practices to fit their perception and approaches.

Bridging Cultures in Early Care and Education (Zepeda, Gonzalez-Mena, Rothstein-Fisch, & Trumbull, 2006) explains two organizing concepts called *individualism* and *collectivism*, which can be used as tools to work with when differences cause conflicts. This particular framework is just one way in which to explore cultural and individual family differences when conflicts arise. In research done on elementary schools (Rothstein-Fisch, 2003; Trumbull, Diaz-Meza, Hasan, & Rothstein-Fisch, 2001), these concepts have been shown to be accessible and highly useful in improving home-school understanding.

When ECE professionals view family priorities and value systems in a nonjudgmental way, they learn not only about other cultures, but about their own as well. Culture, which can be defined as a set of values, beliefs, and ways of thinking about the world that influences everyday behavior (Trumbull & Farr, 2005), passes from one generation to another through childrearing practices. Culture is mostly invisible, except when it bumps up against differences in other values and belief systems through interactions. The two basic concepts—*individualism* and *collectivism*—help make visible how culture influences attitudes, beliefs, values, and behaviors. Each orientation is associated with a different set of priorities that often shows up in care and education practices.

What are the differences between these two patterns? People with a strong individualistic perspective see the importance of children learning that they are unique and special individuals, so the adults stress independence and individual achievement. The focus is on the needs of the individual, self-expression, and personal choice. Physical, emotional, and mental exploration in a safe environment is often a priority. Objects become important as sources of learning about the world and how it works. Adults teach respect for personal possessions.

Although taking the individualistic perspective may seem "normal" or "natural" to you, most of the world's cultures (70% according to Triandis, 1989) and many families in North America have more collectivistic tendencies and place a higher priority on *inter*dependence than on independence. People with a collectivistic perspective are more likely to emphasize group needs over individual needs. Social responsibility is important to people with a collectivistic orientation. They also tend to stress respect for authority and group norms. Personal possessions are downplayed, and human relationships are more important than objects.

APPROACHES

- Remember that the concepts of individualism and collectivism are merely tools and can't be considered more than that. Don't use these tools to oversimplify or categorize people and families. It's important to refrain from stereotyping people or putting them in cultural boxes.

- Also remember that all conflicts over childrearing differences are not cultural ones but can come from a family tradition, an individual experience, specific kinds of training, and philosophical ideals.
- In the face of differing ideas about early care and education practices, seek to establish common ground with individual families and groups of families without simply imposing regulations, rules, and restrictions.
- Look around to see if the program is highly individualistic: The physical environment is also likely to reflect this perspective, with children having their own cubbies, lockers, or coat hooks identified as "theirs" and with their names and pictures prominently displayed. Children are encouraged to take care of their property, take care of themselves (e.g., toileting, feeding, dressing), and use "their words" to identify their wants and needs. All of these examples are signs that individualism is valued.
- Look for the parts of the program that may reflect a more collectivistic orientation, which stresses respect for authority and obligation to group norms. In collectivistic settings, possessions are often shared, with objects being important in the context of human relationships, not in and of themselves. For instance, children may not be urged to play with objects or investigate them independently. In a more collectivistic setting there is more emphasis on the group than on the individual. The collectivistic perspective favors large-group size for activities over small-group or individual interaction, and mixed-aged grouping where older children help and assist the younger children.
- Develop an appreciation for these contrasting patterns of care and education and understand that they need not be mutually exclusive.
- See if you can use these two organizing concepts to figure out how to remain sensitive to each family's needs and wants even when they conflict with your ideas or the program's practices.

Sometimes it looks as though people with a more collectivistic orientation "baby" people. Here is a short story about a woman who enjoyed "babying." Roz, was a family child care provider who emigrated from Taiwan to the United States as a child. Once, in a meeting of early care and education professionals, someone said that it was important not to do anything for a child that the child could do for himself or herself. Roz looked skeptical and quickly said that she disagreed with that statement. She then talked about how her grandmother loved to "baby" her, even after she grew up. Roz felt it was very important that she let her grandmother take care of her because it made the old woman happy. It didn't matter that Roz could do for herself what her grandmother did for her. Roz's response started a whole conversation as various people gave their opinions about independence and interdependence.

Jan, another family child care provider spoke up with passion in her voice. She said that she always hated to be "babied" when she was a child and even more so as an adult. She said that she felt resentment toward people who didn't let her do things by herself.

Like most people, Roz and Jan don't call themselves collectivists or individualists; nevertheless these two have very different viewpoints about being helped or helping themselves. If someone were to observe them working with children and families, it is likely that their two perspectives would have an influence on their behavior.

13 COMMUNICATION: NONVERBAL ACROSS CULTURES

▌ RATIONALE

Nonverbal behavior is like a secret code that is understood but not talked about. Meaning never comes in words alone, but also relates to posture, movement, facial expressions, eye movements, gestures, and how close or how far away we stand. We must be able to pick up silent messages sent with or without words. We all read these messages effectively everyday, except when we meet someone who has a different system of nonverbal communication. That's when miscommunication occurs.

For example, miscommunication may occur when someone from Mexico watches an Anglo explaining a child's height by holding a hand out with the palm down. Although this gesture is easily understood by many people in the United States, a person from Mexico might find it very strange, because that particular gesture is only used for measuring objects. To measure people, the index finger is pointed at the appropriate height. This may not be a big issue, and perhaps will be laughed off by the Mexican person, but nevertheless the message received is different from what was intended.

A bigger issue occurs when a teacher touches a child on the head and the parent worries that the gesture has stolen the child's spirit. Some people from Southeast Asia attach deep significance to a hand on the head. To other people, touching someone on the head is a sign of affection and a way they express love or comfort to dogs or children. Most of those people would never touch adults above the shoulders, however, and would not touch the president of the United States at all except to shake his hand if it were offered. Touching rules are governed by status and power issues and tied into respect. How, when, where, and why we touch each other is cultural. No one explains the rules, but we learn them. Cultural learning is subtle and starts very early.

Touching patterns vary greatly from culture to culture. Touch is just one example of a cultural difference that affects communication. Personal space is another. How close we stand or sit or whether we breathe on people we are talking to holds cultural meanings. A person who comes from a "close culture" feels she is being shunned when someone from a more distant culture backs off. The person backing off may feel crowded and find the experience awkward or offensive. She may even feel afraid. If she feels angry, she may be tempted to say "Get out of my face!" Yet the person who came too close in the name of friendliness may feel the one backing off is weird or is a cold, uncaring person. Each reads the message from the other in a way that is different from what was intended.

Eye contact is another example of cultural difference. Learning about eye contact patterns starts in infancy. For example, in cultures where babies are constantly carried on their mothers' backs, intimacy is not necessarily expressed by eye-to-eye gaze. One common pattern of eye contact in the United States is for the listener to look directly at the speaker and the speaker to gaze briefly into the listener's eyes, then look away. Someone with this pattern who talks to someone with a different eye contact pattern may feel uncomfortable. He may even regard the listener who doesn't look at him as shifty, dishonest, or disrespectful. "Look at me when I talk to you" is sometimes heard from teachers whose students' eye contact patterns don't necessarily match their own. The listener who is expressing respect by keeping his eyes lowered or looking elsewhere when being spoken to may be mystified by the speaker's reaction to this eye contact pattern.

"Don't stare!" is a cultural command to children, but not a universal no-no. In some cultures it's not only polite to stare but expected. A member of a staring culture feels rejected when no one stares at him. In other cultures, staring is not only impolite but can be considered downright dangerous.

APPROACHES

- Become consciously aware of nonverbal behaviors. Although you may be used to reading messages that come from posture, movement, facial expressions, eye movements, gestures, and relative distance, realize that across cultures these behaviors don't necessarily mean the same thing. Look for communication problems below the level of words and their meanings. The goal is to expand your ability to pick up silent messages in ways that they were intended.

- Recognize your own patterns of nonverbal behavior. Most of us are unconscious of these until we meet someone who doesn't fit our patterns. Consider that even though your own may feel right, normal, or good doesn't mean that they are in anyway to superior to other person's nonverbal behavior patterns.

- Recognize that learning unwritten cultural rules of nonverbal communication takes time and patience. The best approach is to be aware of differences and to read the feedback from the parent or family member exhibiting them. Try different approaches if you are picking up discomfort in your attempts to communicate.

- Sometimes you can talk about subtle behavior differences, but it takes sensitivity to bring them out without causing further discomfort and perhaps defensiveness. Having a relationship with the parent or family member you are talking to can help bring the issues to the surface and make it easier to discuss them.

- Don't expect that just because you know a person's culture you can predict his or her behavior. Few cultural patterns are rigid or apply to all members of that culture. Furthermore, cultural patterns change when they come in contact with new patterns.

These two seem to be doing just fine reading each other's nonverbal communication, but they could have a problem if one moves in closer or the other steps back. The amount of personal space an individual feels comfortable with is just one aspect of nonverbal communication.

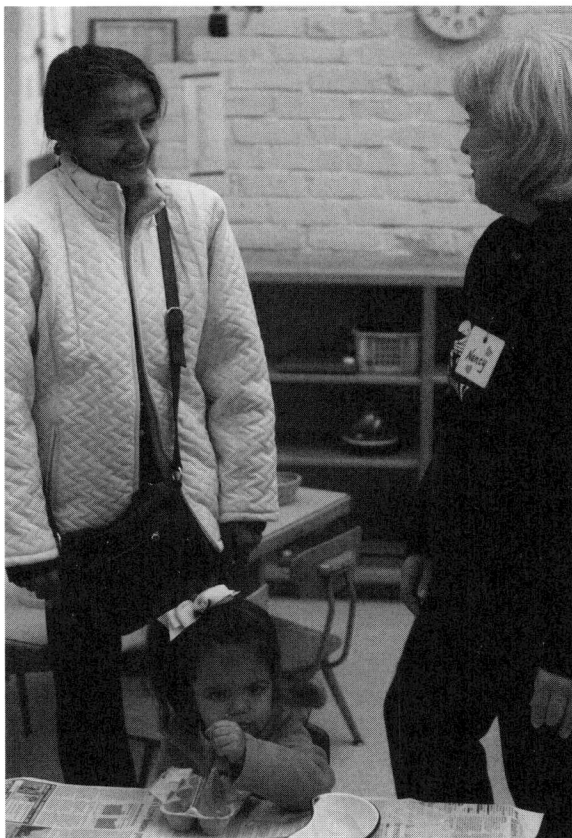

14 COMMUNICATION THROUGH WRITING

RATIONALE

Attempts should be made to communicate with family members in every medium possible. Writing is one major way to get messages across. Throughout the history of early childhood education, teachers and parents have communicated with each other through writing.

Although not yet universal, e-mail messages have become a major way of communicating with some parents. Notes, messages of concern, making appointments, newsletters, articles, and most things that used to go home on paper can now be sent by e-mail. This is especially useful in corporate child care programs, where such communication can be timely and immediate and is especially useful if children and parent are located in the same building. Be considerate about flooding parents with too much—a problem with technology. In the past, the problem was not enough communication; now it is so easy to send an e-mail with an attachment that it is sometimes overdone.

Attempts should be made to communicate with family members in every medium possible. Written notices are one important way to get messages across.

This letter goes home to families the first week of school. It is intended to give them a brief introduction to the classroom to tide them over until Back-to-School Night.

First Grade
Ms. Ritz
Monte Vista School

First grade is an exciting year because children expand their learning incredibly, exert their competence and and develop independence. My goals for all children are to

- support learning by assessing the appropriate activities that will challenge children without discouraging them;
- encourage children to find their strengths so they can feel proud of their accomplishments;
- help children find strategies to become self-motivated learners.

This is a "Can Do" classroom. First graders can do lots of things!

Behavior:

Lifeskills teach children the language of responsible behavior. Our classroom will use Lifeskills, I messages, a Peace Table and Classroom meetings to make sure students have all the knowledge needed for successful behavior.

No one's perfect. On horrible, no good, very bad days, anyone might need some time out. In our class it is called Australia. Children who are sad, angry, etc. can spend a few minutes quietly there to regroup for learning.

For problems between peers the Peace Table is a place to give and receive I messages without disturbing others.

Repeated disruptive behavior that interferes with learning can occur. Children will bring home a Lifeskill Homework note. Please discuss the problem, suggest some strategies or solutions, sign and return.

I'm sure you'll have questions and concerns as time goes on. Please communicate any concerns as they arise. Ask questions, share ideas, offer help. These are ways to get in touch with me:

- You can send a note in your child's folder.
- Leave a post- it on the "moon table" during Family Reading.
- Phone the school: 792–4531.
    If it can't wait until the next day, call my home before 9 pm: 578–8052.
- Send me e-mail: kritz414@sbcglobal.net

Let's have a great year!

APPROACHES

- Use e-mail for those parents who read and respond to e-mail. But don't use it exclusively. Be sure to use other means to get to parents who don't have or don't use e-mail regularly.
- Consider using two-way journals. This written device is especially effective in infant-toddler programs where daily two-way communication is vital in order to meet the child's needs. A two-way journal is used during the day by the staff to record events and details of caregiving, from amounts eaten to diaper contents and changes. Of course, other items of interest can also be included. At the end of the day the journal goes home with the family, who records what caregivers need to know the next day—how well the baby slept, when he or she ate, and any notable differences in routine. Mood changes can be indicators of onset of illness and should be noted as well.
- Use personal notes to communicate about a variety of things. It doesn't take long to jot down a little note on a piece of paper and send it home with the child. Subjects for notes can be positive comments about the child, something he or she did or said, and an appreciation of some contribution he or she made to another or to the class. Of course, thank-you notes to family members for their contributions are not only a social nicety but also let parents know that they are appreciated.
- Happy-grams are commercial notes that are easy to use to send home bits of good news about a child. Usually they have smiley faces and a place to fill in blanks. These can be a real bonus for parents who are used to notes coming home about misbehavior instead of good news.

- The opposite of happy-grams for some families may be assessment reports. For kindergarten and primary students, these may be in the form of report cards or test results. Certainly it's better for any assessment results to be discussed with families in person rather than sent home on a piece of paper, but the reality is that such things do happen. (See Strategy 5, Assessment, for more about this subject.)
- Communicate with families through newsletters. Newsletters help parents know what is going on in the classroom. Having an idea of recent themes, activities, and events helps them talk to their children about their experiences. Newsletters also clue family members in to upcoming events. They can serve as a means of connecting families to each other, especially when they contain news items pertaining to families. Other uses of the newsletters can be to help parents understand the purposes of various activities and give ideas for carrying on themes and activities that originate in the classroom in the home. The newsletters can also ask for ideas or recipes from families; thus, the newsletter becomes a two-way communication device.
- Communicating through the use of bulletin boards is another way of communicating through writing. Some parents who don't interact a good deal with the teacher or staff may use bulletin boards as important sources of information. Here are some ideas for effective bulletin boards:
  - Put bulletin boards in a location where they are clearly visible and accessible.
  - Label the bulletin board so that parents know it is for them. Make it attractive and keep it up to date. If it always looks the same, parents will stop looking at it.
  - Items on the bulletin board should respond to specific interests of the families enrolled.
  - The bulletin board can include such items as recipes for play dough, guidelines in choosing books or toys, announcements of coming events, and community resources.
  - Pertinent articles of interest to parents are useful. If it is a short article, it can just be posted. If it is a longer article, then copies should be available for family members to take home.
- Some programs have a daily bulletin—often hand printed on a white board that give parents the highlights of what went on that day. This bulletin is more timely than a newsletter and more visible than an item on the bulletin board. Such a device can provide parents with conversation starters when they talk to their children. The question "What did you do today?" sometimes is answered "Nothing." It often works better to mention something specific such as "How did you like making tortillas today?"
- Some programs have a parent library and make books and articles available to borrow.
- Some programs collect pamphlets from community resources and make copies available to parents.

A story: One kindergarten had a traveling teddy bear that was accompanied by a journal intended to record his adventures in the homes he visited. The bear and the journal came in a backpack and went home with a different child each weekend. The idea was for a family member to read parts of the journal to the child and help him or her write additional journal entries, which could be dictated by the child and written by the parent.

This communication is designed to involve the parents at home in working on specific skills that the child needs at school.

> To the folks at _____
> house,
>   Your child needs extra practice in
> _____.
> Please spend some time working with your child on this skill. A little attention now will make a big difference later on.
>   Thanks,
>
>   KITTY KITZ

15

COMMUNITY: CREATING A SENSE OF

RATIONALE

Think of a community as a group of people connected by some common interest or purpose. Going by that definition, an early childhood program or classroom can certainly become a community. Sometimes it happens naturally, but usually it takes a little effort to facilitate the making of those connections. It doesn't have to be hard. Think of how a good hostess moves among guests, introducing them to each other and making a group of individuals or couples into a party. Some of the skills a good hostess has apply directly to the goal of forming children, families, and staff into a community. The purpose is different because the main objective is not just a social one, but an enhancement of the children's care and education experience. Also, the focus is longer than a party—not just for an evening but for perhaps a year or more. Sometimes the connections families make with each other in early care and education programs last for a lifetime!

In 1980 Ethel Seiderman cofounded an organization called the Parent Services Project as a way to support families. The idea was to focus on families instead of just on children. In a book about the Parent Services Project, called *Stronger Together*, Lisa Lee (2004) explains the benefits of community building. "One of the gifts of family-centered programs is the creation of caring communities. Connected to one another by their children, adults in such places care about and help one another . . . Families use the center as a place to connect with one another. When good things happen for one family, everyone celebrates. When problems occur, people are concerned and work together . . . in such a place, children grow up feeling safe, covered in a quilt of warmth from the adults in their lives."

So how do early childhood professionals turn a group of people into a community? Seiderman is a master at turning groups into communities, and she has been doing it for a number of years, starting before the Parent Services Project when she was a child care director and ran a family-centered program. Her idea was to support the parents to support the child. That idea is blossoming, partly because of Seiderman's long-time commitment to changing the focus from the child to the family and from the family by itself to the community. Seiderman says that her agency emphasizes the idea that parenting is not just a private concern of the family but a communitywide concern. One way to broaden the parenting role is to give teachers and parents new ways of supporting each other.

Marion Cowee, a preschool director for many years, explains how to create a community from a group of families (Cowee, 2005). "You have to make sure that everybody has a sense of belonging." Cowee doesn't mean just the parents—but suggests "finding out who are the potential members of this community. Include everyone who is important in each child's life, including grandparents, aunts, and nannies." She was clear that the goal is to help everyone feel that they belong in your classroom or program. Marion and long-time toddler and preschool teacher Lynne Doherty contributed to the following list of strategies.

Your attitude makes a difference. If you are trying to build a sense of belonging, you will invite family members in regularly. One way is by having an open-door policy that encourages family members to drop in whenever they want. Some teachers have a strong reaction to that idea and consider it too disruptive. Kitty Ritz, a first-grade teacher, has solved that problem. She sets aside a half hour twice a week at the beginning of the day for family reading time in her classroom. This is one of the many ways that she gets to know the parents and they get to know each other. That's another secret to minimizing disruptions when family members come to visit. Get them involved in productive ways that don't disturb the children. Make them part of the children's routine.

The following are additional ways to create a sense of belonging and make the kinds of connections that turn a group into a community.

APPROACHES

- Create a sense of belonging from the beginning by finding out what everybody with whom you come in contact wants to be called. Then work on learning all the names—including the correct pronunciation. This is not an easy job if the program or class is large, but it is a good way for early childhood professionals to work on their own learning skills as models for the children.
- Introduce everyone who is part of the program or a support to the classroom—such as aides, cooks, custodians, or bus drivers.
- Help people get acquainted by putting up a picture board of the staff with a little something written about each person. It could be a short biography, or a statement about what the person likes about working with children and families, or a list of hobbies. Put this somewhere that families who drop their children off can easily see it. Some programs include substitutes on the picture board as well as regular employees.
- Consider a picture board of families also, with a few facts or statements about each one. Put this up where staff and other families can see it.
- If the entry area has the space, consider not just a bulletin board for parents, planned and maintained by the staff, but also a bulletin board for parents that they themselves plan, maintain, and interact with. An interactive idea to put on the family bulletin board is a changing survey with space for family members to write under a question. For example, a question could be, What is your child's favorite restaurant? This kind of question gives parents something to talk to each other about.
- In a preschool setting, if children arrive with a family member each day, have the room set up for a free play period and make yourself available to greet children and adults. When children enter an interesting environment, they can separate more easily and also become engaged with the materials and each other. That gives adults a chance to talk to each other briefly both at the beginning of the session and at the end. (See Strategy 20 about ongoing conversations with families.)
- Introduce families to each other. Become aware of where personal connections are forming and, later on, suggest that maybe the family would consider changing the emergency form to include new friends to come get the child when necessary, rather than the distant aunt in another town whom the child barely knows.

For family reading time in a first-grade classroom, parents are invited to participate two days a week for the first half hour of the morning.

- Help parents become resources to each other. Carpooling is one way they can work together and gain a sense of belonging to a community.
- Use the intake interview, if there is one, to begin getting acquainted, including finding out what special interests or skills family members might have.
- Make sure your environment is welcoming to everybody. (See Strategy 4, Antibias Environment, for ideas.) A welcoming environment means that images on the walls include everybody, the languages of the families are represented, and adaptations are made for people with disabilities—both children and adults. One program wanted to make sure that all the books they had available for the children gave welcoming messages, so they taped a clean sheet of paper to the inside cover of each book with the suggestion for parents to write their comments and reactions to the book. They found out that what one parent loved, another felt offended by. In this way both parents and staff learned about differing perspectives on what feels welcoming.
- Having an address list is always a good idea—so families can connect with each other on their own. Be sure you have permission from each family to put their name and contact information on the list.
- Fund-raising is a way for family members to get to know each other by working together. Be careful to recognize that some families have children in more than one class or program and fund-raising can get to be a burden in a large family.
- Always think of meetings as a way for people to get to know each other no matter what the purpose of the meeting is. Start with an icebreaker to loosen people up and get them relaxed and interacting. (See Strategy 33 for hints on how to run meetings so that families form relationships with each other.)
- This entire book is full of ideas about how to make families and staff into a community. In particular, look at Strategy 25 for ideas about how to set up the environment for communication, Strategy 26 for ideas about how to get families to participate in the program, and Strategy 37 for ideas about how to build partnerships with families.

A picture board of the families in the program helps to create a welcoming spirit and a feeling of belonging.

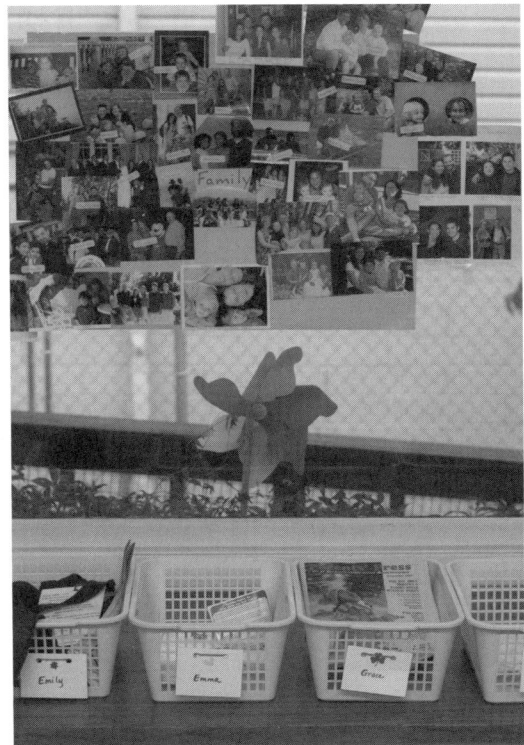

16 COMMUNITY RESOURCES: REFERRALS

RATIONALE

"Child care is a natural meeting place to bring together the needs of children and families and the community resources that they may need to access" (Seiderman, 2003, p. 358). When early care and education programs focus on the sharing of information and resources, everybody benefits. It isn't just the professionals who have information—families also have their own resources that they can share with staff and other families. A sharing spirit makes a difference between a program in which the staff gives and the families receive and one in which giving and receiving are reciprocal. The program becomes a community. (See Strategy 15 about creating a community.) The problem is that it doesn't happen easily. The professionals are busy with the children, and when it comes to resources, they are lucky if they have a list to give out.

A huge question arises with low-income and homeless families. How can teachers and caregivers create partnerships with parents and expect them to be part of their children's care and education if the family's basic needs are not being met? Economic welfare is a vital requirement for food, clothing, and shelter. Families who lack the ability to provide basic needs for their children come to early care and education programs in significant numbers. According to the Children's Defense Fund (2004), "More than 12 million children are poor and millions more live in struggling families with incomes just above the official poverty line." That's 1 out of 6 children (p. 1).

Many of the children in early care and education programs are in single-parent families, and some of those children or family members have disabilities and other kinds of challenges. According to Turnbull and Turnbull (2001), "Those households headed by a single parent who has a child with a developmental disability have the lowest income of any household type" (p. 217).

We won't be able to solve a family's economic problems with the strategies in this chapter, but understanding about family support services can help teachers, caregivers, and providers direct families to the community resources that can help them. From its early beginning, Head Start recognized the importance of connecting the community to their programs and the families to the community. This federally funded program has long served as a model for other programs.

Here is some information about supports for low-income families. The federal program designed to provide economic help is called TANF (Temporary Assistance for Needy Families). Social Security provides income assistance for low-income families who have children with disabilities under SSI (Supplemental Security Income). Medicaid is a federal program providing medical assistance for low-income people. Even though they are underfunded, these three programs can begin to address some of the economic and medical needs. Some states have programs that help to fill in where federal programs have proved to be insufficient.

APPROACHES

- Ethel Seiderman (2003), who heads up an organization called Family Services Project, said, "Community building based on caring relationships encourages optimal availability and use of resources. Accessing resources doesn't happen in a vacuum" (p. 360). She offers some strategies

"Child care is a natural meeting place to bring together the needs of children and families and the community resources that they may need to access" (Seiderman, 2003, p. 358).

for becoming an early care and education program that emphasizes family support services. She suggests:

- ○ Revise your own image of your program to include being part of the economic and human service infrastructure of the community. Network with community leaders.
- ○ Become known and make your voice heard in your community, including attending school board meetings. Become a speaker at social, business, and professional groups in the community.
- ○ Partner with various community organizations so together you are stronger.
- Turnbull and Turnbull (2001) offer some strategies early childhood professionals can use to collaborate for improved economic situations for the families they serve:
  - ○ Make sure that the director, teachers, caregivers, or other staff members know about the potential resources that might help families. Those include TANF; federal Earned Income Tax Credit; state income and other tax credits; food stamps; child support enforcement income, plus child-related resources such as health benefits—Medicaid or state child health insurance program—and child care subsidies.
  - ○ When a program or class includes children with identified disabilities or suspected disabilities, make sure someone on the staff knows about early intervention or special education services.
  - ○ Team up with other community organizations such as domestic violence, mental health, and substance abuse agencies to address prevention and treatment issues for vulnerable families.
  - ○ Increase advocacy along with parents and other groups at both state and local levels to do the following (see also Strategies 1 through 3 on advocacy):
    - ■ Improve the availability of high-quality child care and education that is responsive to family needs.
    - ■ Promote economic and security supports for families while working on a shared agenda focused on families with the most severe barriers to meeting their economic needs.

17 COMPETITION: PARENTS AND PROFESSIONALS

RATIONALE

A huge barrier to a working relationship is a feeling of competition between professionals and families. Sometimes parents observe that their child behaves much better around the teacher or provider than around them. This can make parents feel insecure. It's important that professionals acknowledge to themselves and to the parents that some of the reasons for this difference is less about skills and more about attachment. When children feel insecure and afraid, they may be afraid to act out. As soon as the parent arrives, they once again feel secure and less inhibited. This feeling can result in difficult behavior. Also, the child has a closer relationship with the parent, which means that emotions can be passionate or intense. The child who exhibits only mild anger around the professional can experience a meltdown when the parent is present. It may be that the professional has skills that the parents don't, but these other two reasons need to be taken into consideration.

Another factor is that early childhood practitioners who work with children under age 5 have a poor public image and are called babysitters by some. Couple that situation with low wages and the result may be that the practitioner becomes defensive. As early childhood people seek to establish themselves as true professionals, they may flaunt their knowledge and power. Parents who feel insecure in their parenting competencies may look to the professional as more competent and more knowledgeable than they are.

A very touchy area of competition between parents and professionals is competition for the love of the child—whether such is real or only perceived. This competition can be very damaging to a relationship between the adults. As Jim Greenman and Anne Stonehouse point out (1996), "It is hard not to compete with parents for the child's affections. Caregivers become attached to children and take pleasure in their attachment. . . " (p. 266). Although attachment to adults in the early care and education program is important, especially in younger children, even parents who are aware of that fact may still feel pangs of jealously if they perceive that competition exists.

APPROACHES

- Give credit to families for their funds of knowledge. Even though the early childhood professional may be an expert on children in general, families are the experts on their own children. Both these kinds of expertise need to come together to provide the best care and education for young children.
- Reassure the families that they are number one in the child's life and you are well aware of that fact.
- Be aware of when you might be creating competitive situations.
- Watch out for creating excessive emotional dependence in the children. When children care too much about a teacher, it can be hard on the teacher and on the parents as well.
- Also be aware of your own emotional dependence on the children. One teacher who was absent for two days confessed that she was hurt that the children didn't miss her more than they did.
- Be sensitive to physical affection between yourself and the children if it seems to bother a particular parent.
- Notice any "child-saving" tendencies in yourself. Become aware of any feelings of rescuing the child from the family. That's not unusual in people who work with young children in early care

Are these two competing for this child's attention? It looks like they might be.

and education programs. Sometimes it represents a stage that will pass as the person develops professionally. We can't help our feelings, but we can be honest with ourselves about them and stop ourselves from acting on them.

The following is a story from the author: I remember when I was caught in the grasp of what I think of as a "savior complex." I was a new preschool teacher and was out to save many children from their parents (not all—some parents I approved of—the ones like me). Not only was I in the child-saving business, but I was going to save the whole world through my work with children by raising a generation that was better than the last one. I was definitely riding on a high horse. I am glad to say I moved out of that stage once I realized that parents play a much more important role in children's lives than I ever would, and I needed to team up with them, not look down on them.

18 CONFERENCES

RATIONALE

Conferences are designed to be a structured situation for the exchange of information and plans. They are more formal than the kinds of conversations that occur on a frequent basis between professionals and family members. This should be a time during which information is exchanged freely and questions and ideas are explored. One goal of a conference should be to further relationships, because this is a time when relationships can grow if handled carefully.

Conferences should not just be held to discuss bad news and unacceptable behavior, even though the term *progress report* has just those connotations in some primary programs. Families will start dreading conferences if they don't have any positive experiences with them.

There are many compelling reasons to hold conferences on an ongoing basis instead of just having casual conversations with families. Casual conversations often have audiences, and they get interrupted. Just talking regularly may keep both sides informed about aspects of learning and development on a daily or weekly basis but may not give the overall picture. A conference is the time to focus and concentrate in a private, comfortable setting. If enough time is allowed, questions and concerns can be discussed and misunderstandings can be cleared up. Conferences are good for providing the details as well as the bigger picture of learning and development, and they have the potential to increase knowledge when mutual sharing occurs. Conferences can be the time to discuss goals and plans and work to make sure those of the program are compatible with those of the family.

APPROACHES

- Recognize parents' feelings and expectations around conferences. Their own childhood experience with schools, teachers, and grades can bring up unpleasant memories around parent-teacher conferences. Conferences can also bring up their hopes, as well as their fears.
- Prepare for the conferences by making the purpose clear. If the purpose of the conference is to share information about a child's learning and development, plan ahead about how to do this sharing. Have specific examples of changes in the child since the last conference. Show examples from the child's work and play (including photos or video clips when possible) as well as stories and anecdotes. Be sure you include social and emotional progress as well as physical and cognitive. (See Strategy 5, Assessment.) Collect records of actual incidents that show social-emotional growth. Use storytelling to show progress.
- Conferences should be explained when the family first arrives in the program. If there is a parent handbook, written material about conferences should be included so that parents don't think when asked to attend a conference that something is wrong.
- Schedule conferences so that all families can come. Timing is important. If conferences are only held during the day, some family members may be excluded. If they are held only at night, others may be excluded. Ideally, conference scheduling should be flexible enough so nobody is excluded.
- Open up conferences to any family member who wants to come, and watch out for thinking only of mothers when planning conferences. Fathers may be the most interested party. Sometimes grandparents may be as concerned with what happens at the program or school as the parents.

- Suggest the possibility of observation before the conference. Watching their child in action can help family members see what goes on in the program and how their child relates. It can give them ideas about what to ask or comment on when they get to the conference.
- Think about ways to make family members feel at ease during the conference. Consider the setting and environment. (See Strategy 24, Empowerment, and Strategy 25, Environments for Communication.) Food or drink can help.
- Avoid using jargon. Explain in plain language what you want the parents to understand. Jargon puts you above the family and makes you an expert. You may be an expert, but so are the parents. Don't let expertise get in the way of communication or the relationship you should be building with each family.
- Don't compare children to other children or to charts. Be careful of saying words like *fast*, *slow*, *behind*, or *ahead*. Growing up is not a race. Be aware of which words trigger feelings. *Normal* is a trigger word and *abnormal* is even more of one. *Typically* or *atypically developing* are better terms. Talk about challenges rather than problems. Avoid labels or judgmental words; instead use objective ways of talking about children—describe behaviors rather than labeling them.
- Check out your attitude. (See Strategy 7, Attitudes of Professionals.) Make sure that you and the parent are on the same side, figuratively and literally.
- Make sure that the conversation is two-way, not just a monologue on the part of the professional.
- Know your limits. Don't assume that you can be everything to every family. Don't expect that you have the solution to every situation. Don't stretch your knowledge and experience beyond their boundaries. Sometimes you need to bring in or refer parents to other resources. (See Strategy 16, Community Resources.)
- Respect confidentiality. Gossip is unprofessional, even when it is not harmful. Don't talk about one family to another.

Forms such as these may be used for the beginning-of-the-year conferences. Parents have the opportunity to express the dreams, wishes, and needs of their children at conferences held during the first month of school. Responsibility is shared by parent, student, and teacher.

Conferences are designed to be a structured place to exchange information and make plans. They are more formal than the kinds of conversations that occur on a frequent basis between professionals and family members.

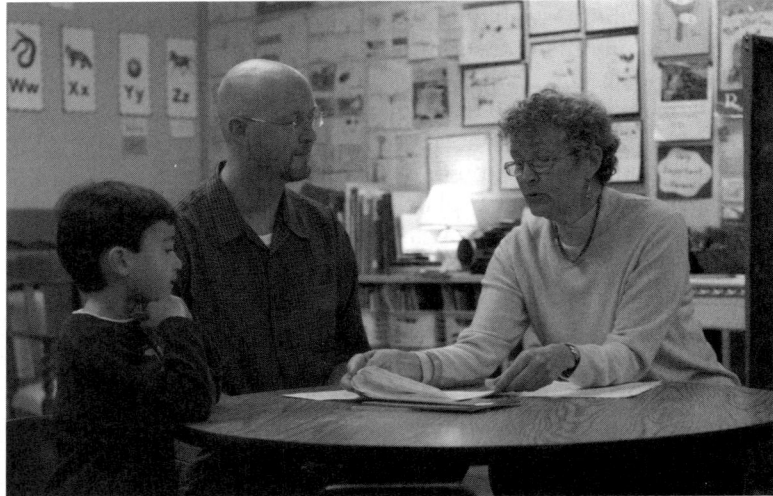

- Help parents to problem solve, but don't expect problems to be solved quickly or neatly. Your role is to help parents sort things out if they ask you for solutions or advice. You can share your knowledge and experience, but they need to come to their own conclusions.

A story: Four-year-old Kai was playing by himself on the floor with blocks and small figures. His voice could be heard across the room, talking nonstop. He manipulated the figures creating dramatic action while they talked loudly to each other. Kai placed two figures on top of a block tower and one was hanging down on a rope. The two on top kept looking at the dangling one and they were having a loud argument when the teacher announced that it was kaie for a snack. Kai didn't stop playing. A few minutes later the teacher approached him and insisted that he come to the snack table. "Awww," he protested. "Do I have to put things away?" he asked. "No, you can put a 'save sign' on what you have there" was the teacher's response. "Yeah," he said, "But I'll forget where I am." He looked forlornly at the two figures on top and the dangling one. "I'm sorry," said the teacher, "but you have to come now." Kai's face showed his distress, and he hung his head while folding his arms defiantly. Suddenly he looked up at the teacher and smiled. "I know what," he said confidently. "I'll just start a new episode." When the teacher told Kai's parents about this situation during a conference, they could see how their son was maturing. They were surprised that he used a word like episode, especially since they had no TV at home. They knew he had a great imagination, that wasn't a surprise, but this was the first time his teacher had paid close attention to just how well he could play alone. The best thing about this story for both parents and the teacher was that it showed how Kai was making progress in coping with transitions.

19 CONFERENCES: CROSS-CULTURAL

RATIONALE

The information in Strategy 18 on conferences also applies in cross-cultural situations. In addition, other barriers to communication may need to be addressed. The first one may concern time concepts and what it means to be late. For some people, being early is important, so that when the appointed time comes they are already there and waiting. For others, the goal is to walk in the door one minute before the scheduled time. They don't like to wait. For others, forgivably late means 5 or so minutes. Some people don't consider 20 minutes after the scheduled time as truly late. Then for some people, clock time has very little meaning and appointments may have even less. In their culture, arriving several hours or even days after the appointed time is within the bounds of courtesy.

Greetings have cultural rituals associated with them. Do you shake hands or not? What does a firm handshake mean? Does it mean you are a straightforward, competent person or does it mean you are aggressive or rude? It depends on your culture. What does a slight touch mean in a handshake? Are you a weak person with limp hands or are you shaking hands in the polite manner of your culture? What about eye contact? Are you respectful if you look someone in the eye or are you disrespectful? It depends on your culture. Along with culture are gender issues. What is okay for men to do may not be okay for women.

If you want to be warm and friendly, do you smile and insist on being called by your first name? Do you call others by their first name? How you are received depends on the cultural meaning others have to your warm, friendly gestures. Instead of seeing you as open and welcoming, they may feel uncomfortable or think you disrespectful.

Do you like to get right down to business once the conference begins? For some people, it's important to socialize before getting to the point of the conference. Personal information about the family and each member may signal good manners for one family but feel uncomfortably intimate for another.

Of course, a huge barrier arises when families and professionals don't speak the same language. Strategy 18 on conferences addresses this issue when it relates to professional jargon, but that is a minor barrier compared to the one that presents itself when there is no common language between the program and the home.

One solution to these barriers is to become an anthropologist; however, even anthropologists don't understand all the cultural differences that may emerge in one center, family child care, or school.

APPROACHES

- See yourself as a lifelong learner. Studying differences may help, but the best approach is to tune up your sensitivity. There is always more happening than appears on the surface of any interaction, even between two people of the same culture and language group. The meanings of behaviors are what is important and what you need to find out in order to be a good cross-cultural communicator. Observe, ask, read, listen, and discuss to find out which behaviors mean what to which people. The meanings may be cultural, but they may also be individual.

- Be prepared to make mistakes. You will make lots of mistakes. That's the way we learn. Regard each one as a learning situation rather than a failure on your part.
- Assume responsibility for understanding all parents by finding translators, if needed, rather than expecting them to bring their own translators. Be sure the translators are good ones. Also, make sure to provide all written notices in the languages of the families in your program.
- If family members speak your language somewhat but are embarrassed about their skills, help them understand that you are in the same or a worse situation regarding their language. It's important not to assume attitudes of superiority.
- When necessary, give up your agenda and really listen to the parent—not only the words but the feelings behind them. Listen until the person stops talking. Don't interrupt. When it's your turn, instead of arguing, educating, or responding from your own perspective, try to state the perspective of the other person. Put the gist or spirit of what you heard into words by making a statement about the other person's feelings, experience, perceptions, beliefs, or concepts. See if you can get at the deeper message. Most people do little of this kind of listening and responding. In a conversation where there is disagreement, most people constantly push forward their own point of view. Listening skills can be learned. Best of all is the feedback you get when you've received the message someone was trying to send because the communication opens up and the conversation continues.
- Connect parents from the same language backgrounds so they can help and support each other. Also introduce them to family members from other language backgrounds. Don't let language differences keep you from inviting all parents to participate in the program at whatever level they feel comfortable.

The following is a story about differences in time concepts: A visiting professor arrived to teach a class in a country where time had a very different meaning. The first day he arrived in class a few minutes early and only one student was there. By the time the class was supposed to start, he had only a handful of students. "They'll be here," one of the early birds assured him. The class drifted in for the first hour, and eventually the room filled up. The professor worried that he didn't have the full time period he had prepared for. When it was 5 minutes before the end of the class, the professor expected the students to start closing their notebooks and picking up their backpacks. Five minutes later when the clocked clicked onto the closing time, not a single student had made a move to get ready to go. The class continued on for quite some time after the scheduled stopping time. The professor had a whole different time sense to get used to.

20 CONFLICT MANAGEMENT

RATIONALE

Though the long-term goal of conflict management is to resolve the conflict, the immediate and ongoing goal should be to keep from destroying the relationship while trying to reach consensus. The key to both goals is effective communication. Communication is a huge subject and is woven throughout this book. This particular strategy is aimed at looking how to take two seemingly opposite points of view and figuring out what to do that will work for everybody. An approach taken by Isaura Barrera (2003), a professor of special education at the University of New Mexico, involves what she calls *third space.*

Third space has to do with moving from dualistic thinking to holistic thinking in the face of what seems to be a contradiction or a paradox. If a parent toilet trains her baby at 6 months and the policy of the center is to wait until after the second birthday, that situation can create a conflict. Both parties have reasons for what they are doing. The caregiver may think "I'm right and she's wrong." The parent may think the opposite. If they argue, it's the center that will probably win if the parent perceives the caregiver (backed by the director) to be more powerful. If either caregiver or director quotes experts or cites research, doing so will also probably tip the balance in favor of the center. However, parents who lose arguments aren't likely to feel like partners with their child's caregiver.

Aiming for third-space solutions means that conflicts move beyond winning and losing, relationships flourish, and nobody has to give in. The idea of everybody winning in the face of a conflict flies in the face of logic for many Western thinkers, who are used to competitive situations in which there is always a loser. Another factor that can get in the way of reaching a third-space solution is what could be called a blind spot. The problem with blind spots is that we don't know we have them. As I once said to a friend who has tunnel vision—while I was trying to grasp what it must be like, "So is it like looking through two paper towel tubes and everything else is black?" He laughed and said to me, "Janet, what I don't see out of the corners of my eyes is exactly like what you don't see out of the back of your head!" My friend has a blind spot and so do I, but I never think about it.

So what does tunnel vision have to do with this conflict over toilet training? Let's say that the caregiver has knowledge and experience when it comes to toilet training. She is confident in her approach. When faced with a parent whose ideas clash with her expertise, she judges the parent to be wrong, because she has a blind spot that she is unaware of. She is missing a whole piece of what toilet training means to this parent. She considers the parent's approach to be a *problem.* If told the conflict should end in a win-win solution, she feels stuck in the face of a paradox. How can she solve this problem? In order to be culturally sensitive, does she have to give in to something she feels is ridiculous, wrong, or even harmful?

No! Barbara Rogoff (2003) says, "Understanding different cultural practices does not require determining which *one* way is 'right' (which does not mean that *all* ways are fine). With an understanding of what is done in different circumstances, we can be open to possibilities that do not necessarily exclude each other. Learning from other communities does not require giving up one's own ways. It does require suspending one's own assumptions temporarily to consider others and carefully separating efforts to understand cultural phenomena from efforts to judge their value. It is essential to make some guesses as to what the patterns are, while continually testing and open-mindedly revising one's guesses. *There's always more to learn*" (p. 14).

It is likely that the approach to toilet training that this parent is taking is related to cultural or family traditions and has patterns of meaning that the caregiver doesn't understand. (See Strategy 12 for examples of differing patterns of meaning.) Knowing that there are reasons for what the parent is doing that are valid in her mind may still not bring comfort to the caregiver when facing the paradox of two seemingly incompatible approaches.

Parker Palmer (1997) gives advice about how to look at the positive side of paradox. He writes: "We split paradoxes so reflexively that we do not understand the price we pay for our habit. The poles of a paradox are like the poles of a battery: hold them together, and they generate the energy of life; pull them apart, and the current stops flowing. When we separate any of the profound paired truths of our lives, both poles become lifeless as well. Dissecting a living paradox has the same impact on our intellectual, emotional, and spiritual well-being as the decision to breathe in without ever breathing out would have on our physical health" (p. 64).

"Paired truths" is a useful term when working to see a paradox as positive, but the caregiver still has the problem with the parent who believes and does something quite different from what caregiver believes and from the policies of the program.

Barrera and Corso (2003) give some insight into how to use third space in this situation. "A third space perspective does not 'solve the problem.' Rather it changes the arena within which that problem is addressed by increasing the probability of respectful, responsive, and reciprocal interactions. In so doing, an optimal response to the situation becomes more likely" (p. 81).

Bredekamp and Copple (1997) explained third space without naming it in the second edition of *Developmentally Appropriate Practice in Early Childhood Programs*. They said, "Some critical reactions to NAEYC's (1987) position statement on developmentally appropriate practice reflect a recurring tendency in the American discourse on education: the polarizing into *either/or* choices of many questions that are more fruitfully seen as *both/and*" (p. 23).

Bredekamp and Copple are writing about dualistic thinking, where contrasting ideas are looked at as dichotomous. If it's right, it can't be wrong; if it's bad, it can't be good. If it's blue, it can't be yellow. When you move into holistic thinking from dualistic thinking, you don't separate differences into opposites. An example of holistic thinking is to bring blue and yellow come together to make green! Blue keeps its blueness and yellow keeps its yellowness, and together they make something new altogether. Green is an example of third space.

APPROACHES

- The first step in working toward consensus around an area of conflict is to suspend judgment and try to understand the other person's perspective. Barbara Rogoff (2003) writes: "We must separate *understanding of patterns from judgments of their value*. If judgments of value are necessary, as they often are, they will thereby be much better informed if they are suspended long enough to gain some understanding of the patterns involved in one's own familiar ways as well as in the sometimes surprising ways of other communities" (p. 14). (See Strategy 12 about patterns.)
- To suspend judgment, take the advice of Rumi, a 13th century poet, who wrote: "Out beyond ideas of wrongdoing and rightdoing there lies a field. I will meet you there." If you go out to that field with a parent to talk about your views, you may be able to see a reality that is bigger than both of you.
- Appreciate the energy of paired truths and remember that to only adhere to one of them is like breathing in without breathing out, according to Parker Palmer (1997). Instead of trying to solve the problem right away, go out to Rumi's field, which changes the arena in which you can have a dialogue.
- Seek an optimal response to the situation and at the same time increase the depth and strength of the relationship. This approach makes it easier to figure out what to do about your differences in this situation, with this child and family in this program. Steven Covey in his foreword to *Crucial Conversations* (Patterson et al., 2002) uses the term *synergy* to label third space. He says it is imperative that we nourish our relationships and develop tools, skills, and enhanced capacity to find new and better solutions to our problems. These newer, better solutions will not represent "my way" or "your way"—they will represent "our way."

- Recognize that to reach a third-space or synergistic solution you need to:
  - Believe it possible.
  - Accept that there are multiple realities and paired truths.
  - Change from arguing and persuading to dialoguing.
- Practice using dialoguing instead of arguing, because according to Steven Covey, genuine dialogue "*transforms* people and relationships . . . and creates an entirely new level of bonding producing what Buddhism calls 'the middle way'—not a compromise between two opposites on a straight-line continuum, but a higher middle way, like the apex of a triangle."

A story: Once, in a workshop, the issue of differences in ideas about toilet training came up. I said, "You don't have to do what the parent wants. It's hard in a center, and I'm just telling you to be respectful of the difference." As I finished the sentence, a hand shot up from the audience. A participant was obviously very eager to speak. She stood up and said, "Here's what happened to me. A mother brought her 1-year-old daughter to the center for the first time, and she told me that she was already toilet trained. I didn't believe her, but instead of responding negatively, I asked her to show me what she did. She showed me and it worked! The baby was trained and didn't need to wear diapers. It didn't take any more time and energy than changing diapers would have." What surprised me about this story was that the participant, though willing to try something new, really didn't have faith that it would work. She was wrong. It did work. This story illustrates a win-win solution. The caregiver kept on with what she believed in for the other children, but was also able to satisfy the mother. In other words, the caregiver expanded her ideas about what was possible and didn't give up anything.

The first step in working toward consensus when conflict surfaces is to suspend judgment and try to understand the other person's perspective. Is that what the woman with the glasses in her hand is doing? Maybe.

21

CONVERSATIONS:
ONGOING—WITH FAMILIES

RATIONALE

Finding time to talk with families is not an easy task for early childhood professionals. When parents arrive with their children and come back to pick them up, it's a busy time for everybody. However, this is the time you see families face to face. It's not the best time of the day, if parents are in a hurry or come back tired, but you can't wait for the perfect opportunity. You may also be busy with other children.

Daily conversations are important in getting to know each other. In many programs, these conversations are the main form of parent involvement and serve an important function of making the parent a part of the program. It can be a time to exchange information on child- and family-related issues.

Not every school sees parents on a daily basis, but some have a policy that a family member take their child to the classroom so that there is daily contact between the teacher and the family member. When family members don't come to school or to the program, telephone conversations can supplement face-to-face contact. Use them to ask about absenteeism or to share a personal observation or anecdote about a child. Although it may be difficult to accept calls from families during working hours, letting them know when are the best times to call gives them the possibility of initiating a conversation. Some teachers make themselves available for telephone conversations on a regular basis and let families know when that is. Nap time is a favorite among preschool teachers.

APPROACHES

- Greet parents by name every time you see them and make a point to say good-bye. If you can squeeze conversation in after the greeting or before the good-bye, parents will feel more valued. That's the way to grow a relationship.
- Make positive remarks about their child whenever you talk to the parents.
- If the child is present, include him or her in the conversation. It's disrespectful to talk around a child as if he doesn't exist.
- The attitude of the professional gives messages about whether it's okay to have a conversation or if this is just a quick encounter. Try to unbusy yourself when family members arrive. It isn't easy when you have a group of children you are responsible for, but it is worth doing.
- If you have problems making yourself available for more than a hello and good-bye, try to figure out a way to do so. Make yourself available, even if it isn't easy. Some ways to do this are the following:
  - Stagger arrival and departure, if possible, so everybody doesn't arrive at once.
  - Have an extra staff person come in during the times that parents are there.
- Suggest that parents visit or observe and then make time to talk to them.
- Although some teachers separate their private lives from their professional lives, others who live in the same neighborhood take time to talk when they run into family members of the children in their center, family child care home, or school.
- Consider home visits if parents are comfortable with them.

Keeping in touch with families through regular conversations with them is important. It isn't always easy to find time, but this director is making time for a quick chat with a mother.

- Schedule conferences and meetings with families, individually or with groups.
- Keeping records of contacts with parents help professionals discover if they are neglecting some families.

A story: A lonely grandfather who came to pick up his granddaughter stayed and stayed. The family child-care provider had to move him toward the door so she could get on with her work. One day he remarked about the piano in the provider's family room. She asked if he played, and he replied that he did. She invited him to play something for the children. After that he came on a regular basis and stayed for a half hour playing for the children. Eventually, he started giving lessons to some of the children. Everybody was happy about the arrangement!

22 CULTURALLY RESPONSIVE CARE AND EDUCATION

RATIONALE

Why culturally responsive care and education? Children are adaptable; can't they just learn new ways of doing things? Besides, doesn't it make sense to aim to create bicultural people? Shouldn't that be a goal of education? What if parents, both immigrants and nonimmigrants, want their children to learn what they consider the "American way" and don't want their practices at home and/or their home language to be part of the program or school? These are all questions that come up in discussions of culturally responsive care and education.

Let's start with the last one first. It's true that parents may make a big separation between what goes on at home and what goes on at school or in early care and education programs. For example, at university lab schools, the foreign students who enroll their children often express the desire for their children to learn English and experience "American culture." They know that they will return to their own country, and they see the potential for their young children to go back home bilingual and with an understanding of a culture different from their own. They don't see a risk factor for their children losing their language or becoming alienated from their own culture.

That's a different situation from an immigrant family who has chosen to come to this country for whatever reason, or a refugee family who ended up here but never chose to come, or a family that has been on this continent for many generations but came involuntarily, or an indigenous family who has been here countless generations. Each of these families may have widely differing ideas about what they want for their children and what part their home language and culture should play in their child's education and development.

Imagine two families coming into a program. One has recently fled from a country where they enjoyed high socioeconomic status and both parents are well educated. Though they are now poor, they have a different set of hopes and expectations from the second family, who arrived three generations ago, have made their living as farm workers, and have children who still speak their home language. There is no way to generalize about the hopes and dreams these families have for their children without asking them. But the answers to the rest of the questions in the first paragraph may be pertinent to their separate situations.

The answers to the rest of those questions fall into several themes. One is identity formation. Another is keeping connections to families strong.

The younger the child, the more unformed is his or her identity. The questions to be answered in terms of identity formation are who am I and where do I belong. According to J. Ronald Lally (1995), "Culture is the fundamental building block of identity. Through cultural learning, children gain a feeling of belonging, a sense of personal history, and security in knowing who they are and where they come from. The child care experience should be in harmony with the culture of the home. Therefore, caregivers should pay great attention to incorporating home practices into care."

Look at feeding as an example of a practice that can have implications for identity formation for babies. In a child care program, children are encouraged to practice self-help skills from early on. That means when babies are old enough to eat finger food, they are given the chance to do so. One parent in the center has a strong reaction to arriving one day to find her child fingering pasta in tomato sauce and making a big mess. In this family, no one ever touches food with their fingers—even sandwiches are eaten with a knife and fork. The lessons in acceptable behavior their baby receives at the center are diametrically opposed to what the family teaches at home. Phillips and Cooper (1992) said, "Feeding has patterns of meaning that are shared by and embodied in the lifestyles of a larger

54

group" (p. 11). So instead of explaining the importance of early self-help skills to this family, a better approach would be for the caregiver to try to understand the patterns of meaning their approaches to eating relate to. (See Strategy 20, Conflict Management, and Strategy 12, Care and Education Practices: When Conflicts Arise.)

Here's another example for older children that could have implications for the child's experience at home. A second-grade teacher is trying to get children to think for themselves. She feels the basis of a democratic society is for children to learn to question authority. To that end, she sometimes makes mistakes on purpose to see if the children will correct her. At home, one child is taught respect for her elders, and the teacher's goals are in direct contrast to her family's. She did fine at first, until she began bringing school behavior home. She began to question older family members, which caused a good deal of dissension in the family. Then she began to disagree with them. The whole household was disrupted by this new behavior.

Both the caregiver and the teacher in these two examples need to communicate with family members and together discuss whether the programs should become more culturally responsive and just how to do it. Such discussions might not be easy. (See Strategy 20, Conflict Management, for further ideas about how to proceed with the discussions.)

APPROACHES

- Listen to what parents want for their children. Go beyond their first statements. Discuss with them the deeper aspects of their dreams and desires for their children. Ask about what they know about other people's experiences. Discuss biculturalism and bilingualism. You can't automatically understand a family by putting them in some broad category—like immigrant. You have to get to know them.
- Learn more about identity formation. Become aware of what messages you are sending to individual children about what is appropriate and what is inappropriate. Think about how your messages are influencing each child's sense of self, sense of cultural competence, and feelings of belonging.
- Reflect on your own early years and your identity formation. How did you gain a sense of self, learn what culture you belonged to, fit in with your family? Do you have some leftover feelings about what happened to you? Identity formation is a subject that some teachers, caregivers, and providers have never thought about before. Knowing oneself can help you better understand others.

23 DECISION-MAKING BOARDS AND COUNCILS: PARENTS' ROLES IN

RATIONALE

In some programs, family members are on an advisory board or council and in some they are the policymakers. Head Start is an example of a model that involves parents at all levels, including giving them an advisory role and to some extent a decision-making role. In parent participation preschools, the parent board is the decision-making body. Of course, not all programs give parents this kind of power. For many the family council is purely advisory, and professionals make the final decisions. Having families in these roles means that the program is more likely to be responsive to their children in the ways they wish. Community connections can be greater when parents are involved in advising and policy setting. The program is more likely to be a firmer part of the community in which the families live and be responsive to its needs. Playing these roles helps parents and other family members see that they can influence what happens in their children's lives. The benefits go beyond their own children when they develop and hone leadership skills that serve their communities.

When families serve on boards and councils, they have a greater voice than when they come as individuals and ask that the program be sensitive to what they want for their children. It often happens that the teachers and staff in a program are from a different culture or socioeconomic level than the families they serve. They apply what they know and believe using the principles and practices they've learned in their teacher preparation courses. Those same principles and practices may set them apart from the families they serve, and communication may be blocked. (See Strategies 12, 20, and 22.) Parent voices are usually quiet when they come individually—and even the loud ones eventually move on to the next grade or program. Having parent boards and councils allows voices to be heard in a different way and provides continuity as well as flexible responsiveness as the board changes over time.

Parent boards and councils benefit caregivers, directors, staff, and teachers as well because they broaden their views as they come to understand perspectives that may be different from their own. When the council or board is working well, professionals enjoy additional support that they might not otherwise experience.

Encouraging leadership among the families served will bring rich rewards. You have to get to know the families well enough to begin to discern leadership qualities. What are those qualities? How do you know a leader when you see one? According to Debra Sullivan (2003), "Leaders are any individuals who influence others in a way that encourages them to higher or better performance and personal development. Effective leaders may or may not have authority, position, or status. They do, however, have integrity, dignity, and respect for others. Leaders empower, encourage, and support others in a shared effort to achieve goals or create change. . . . They take action where action is needed and they enable others to take action when another person's strengths and ability are needed" (p. 7).

APPROACHES

- Help each family understand how the program, organization, or school works so that they have a bigger picture than they would if only tuned into their own and their child's experiences with the caregiver, staff, or teacher.

This advisory group of parents and teachers meets regularly throughout the school year. This particular meeting focused on spending some money that was allocated for school improvement.

> Sunny Valley School
> May 13
>
> Minutes of the Sunny Valley School Site Council meeting held on May 12.
>
> In attendance: Sharon Allen, Latanya Miller, Sandy Smith, Dena Mundy, Sage Johnson, Dean Ames, and Juana Gomez.
>
> The meeting was called to order at 3:39 by Chairperson Juana Gomez. Minutes of the April 14th meeting of the School Site Council were read and approved.
>
> Latanya Miller presented the Council with two copies of the District Mater Plan for School Improvement which outlines the regulations regarding all aspects of school improvement. The district has asked the site council for input concerning possible changes in the Master Plan. Site Council members were asked to review the plan and make appropriate suggestions.
>
> Ms. Miller indicated that the School Improvement Plan budget project for the next year is $14,501, approximately 4,000 less than this year's budget. She also noted that the future of the program is still uncertain.
>
> After a review of the district philosophy relating to student behavior, the Council discussed and composed a discipline plan for use at Sunny Valley School. The plan outlines area of responsibility for students, parents, teachers and administrators.
>
> Ms. Miller distributed copies of the School-wide Environment component composed by the Council at the April meeting.
>
> The meeting was adjourned at 4:43.
>
> Dean Ames,
> Secretary

- Look at your own attitudes. (See Strategy 7.) Openness to parents' perspectives is essential for working with parent boards and councils.
- Learn to look for leadership qualities, even in shy, quiet people. Who has vision? Who wants to make something happen? Who has influence on others? Who can work both independently and interdependently? These qualities may not show up readily. You may have to look hard for them, but you will be richly rewarded as you become increasingly aware of people with leadership potential among the families.
- Mentor new leadership. Encourage and give support to these potential leaders. Provide training for them. Head Start is known for developing leaders—not only in the program, but in the community. A common Head Start story is the bringing up of parents through the ranks of the profession, starting as a parent volunteer and eventually becoming a staff member, a teacher, even working up to director or other administrative position.

Part of the process of creating a board or council is recruiting parents. Parent voices are usually quiet when they come individually—and even the loud ones eventually move on to the next grade or program. Having parent boards and councils allows voices to be heard in a different way and provides continuity as well as flexible responsiveness as the board changes over time.

24 EMPOWERMENT

RATIONALE

What does empowerment mean? That depends on your definition of power. If you equate power with control and domination, then empowerment doesn't make sense. To consider a different definition, look to the origins of the word *power*, which comes from the Latin root meaning *to be able*. Looking down that path brings one to the idea of what is sometimes called personal power. Personal power can be defined as the ability to be who you really are. Intisar Shareef, a community college professor, takes personal power a step further and defines it as the ability to define your own reality and have others accept it. Her definition takes power beyond the personal and into the interpersonal, indeed into the political realm. I see personal power as what is behind interpersonal and political power. All these aspects of power are important, and none need have anything to do with domination.

Watch closely interactions between two people; sometimes their body language tells you that one is trying to dominate the other. Here is an example of such an interaction. A parent storms into the director's office after pushing aside a secretary who tries to stop him. He strides across the room and stands with his hands on the director's desk. He leans way over so his face is close to hers and says, "My child is a vegetarian and your teachers are feeding her meat!" His expression bristles with rage as he waits for her response. Note how both his verbal and nonverbal communication put him in the top dog position—just like in a real-life dog fight where one dog dominates the other. This human interaction is about winning and losing. The parent is out to win the fight and, depending on how the director responds, he just may intimidate her enough to consider himself the winner. This may be dog nature, but it isn' t human nature—it is learned. Anything that is learned can be unlearned. Empowering parents and other family members is about helping them find and use their personal and interpersonal power and helping them avoid using dominant and submissive behaviors.

Some people enjoy jockeying for power. Two people who are equally good at playing the dominating game may switch positions throughout an interaction, leaving no clear winner at the end. Even if one wins, the loser may enjoy the game enough to keep playing it next time they interact. Other people don't jockey for position but immediately make themselves submissive when interacting with someone who is even a little dominating. Look at how that works. The issue is the same, but it is a different parent—a mother comes in to the office after learning that her vegetarian child is being given meat in the child care center. She stops at the secretary's desk and asks to see the director. The secretary says that the director is on the phone and that she will have to wait in the hall outside the office because there is no room for her inside. The mother retreats to the hall and finds the only chair there is a child's chair. She sits down on it. After 15 minutes she checks with the secretary, who apologizes for forgetting her and ushers her into the director's office. The director sits behind a rather large desk reading some papers and doesn't look up when the mother enters. The mother stands shifting her weight from foot to foot. The director finally looks up, paper still in hand, and murmurs, "Yes?" before looking back down at the paper. The person with the power in this situation is the director. We don't know if the mother made herself submissive or was forced into the role by the secretary and director's actions. If being the underdog is her usual role, it' s possible that she'll switch roles in interactions with people she perceives as weaker than herself—such as children.

APPROACHES

- Recognize that the domination system is not natural but is learned. Furthermore, the system is supported by the institutions of the society. That means that not everyone is born with the same chance to win in the domination game. Groups targeted for bias on the basis of race, culture, gender, age, class, ability, or sexual orientation have a harder time dominating than those who enjoy the privileges that the society automatically gives them. Not that all people in nontargeted groups play the domination game, but if they do, it is easier for them to win than people in targeted groups, especially if those in the targeted groups have internalized their oppression. Of course, not all people in targeted groups submit to domination. Many are outstanding game players, but even if they are good enough to win, institutionalized bias makes sure that they never get in a position to play the dominating game with those who control the institutions. Until we all recognize how the domination system operates and work to dismantle it, we won't be fully effective at empowering children and their families.

- What professionals can do is help family members tap into their personal power—the form of power that everyone has. When personal power is acknowledged and nourished, people are able to show who they really are. They don't need to dominate others, and they can resist being put in a submissive position through internalized oppression (where the messages of the oppressor guide the person from the inside).

- Help family members "find their voice," which is the way people express their personal power.

- Empower yourself. Start by becoming aware of how you react to perceived threats by becoming defensive. If the director in the story above had responded to the dominating father by meeting him head on or putting up a protective shield, the result would have been blocked communication. If instead she brought her personal power to the situation, she could have responded as her authentic self and given a nondefensive reaction, perhaps surprising the father out of his dominating stance.

25 ENVIRONMENTS FOR COMMUNICATION

RATIONALE

An environment influences behaviors as well as shapes thoughts and creates feelings in people—adults and children. We behave one way in a library, another way in a bank, a different way in a workout room, and yet another way in a place of worship. The environment gives us messages about how to behave. Part of growing up is learning to read those messages. Early childhood professionals are aware of this phenomenon and often take care to arrange their environments so that children get the right messages about how to behave there. Take an infant center, where exploration is the goal in the play space—the room is set up to encourage such behaviors. Or a library space in a classroom, where the goal is to settle down and enjoy books—the area is set up to be comfortable, cozy, relaxed, and relatively quiet. How much time and energy do early childhood professionals take to set up environments to invite parents into their spaces?

The most likely place to see environmental arrangements made for parents in an infant center or preschool is where family members deliver their children and pick them up. For example, in an infant center, if there is a place for breastfeeding mothers to feel relaxed and comfortable, the message is that they are welcome to come in to feed their babies. In any program, the entry space can give a welcoming message. If the space is limited, it might be a simple message such as a bulletin board with pertinent items displayed. Some programs have cubbies for family members for messages or notices. Of course, a couple of comfortable chairs, a table, a coat rack, and a steaming coffee pot (out of reach of the children) are other welcoming devices. For parents who bring younger siblings with them to pick up their children, some simple toys or baby books readily available say welcome to other family members too. If parents spend time in the program itself, either as observers or as volunteer helpers, another welcoming sign is a place for parents to safely store their belongings.

Many things work against inviting parents through environmental means besides lack of space or funding for adult furniture. If children are bused, the families may not come on a daily basis but only for enrollment procedures, conferences, meetings, or open houses. The spaces for these events may be functional and not very warm and welcoming. That's the common situation. This chapter hopes you'll think beyond what is in order to start conceiving of what can be. Until early childhood professionals raise their sights and begin to envision better spaces than are the norm, there isn't much hope for change. Much of this book is based on visions and hopes for change.

APPROACHES

- Analyze the environment you are in right now and think about how it affects your behaviors, thoughts, and feelings.
- Analyze the early childhood environment you are most familiar with to figure out what messages it may be giving parents. Try to imagine yourself as a parent bringing your child into the classroom. Think about what environmental arrangements could be made to make you feel welcome.
- Help parents get to know the staff of the center or the classroom by putting up a bulletin board with pictures of anyone who works with their children. Include their names, what they want to be called, and short biographical information. Getting to know who is in and around their child's classroom helps parents feel more secure and at home.

Although this is the area where the staff stores their children's books, it serves double duty as a space where adults can get away and talk in private. The adult-size furniture offers more comfort than small chairs, and the round table gives the two a chance to sit closer to each other.

- If parents only come occasionally, be sure that when they do come they feel welcome in the spaces they visit. Put some thought into those spaces.
- Consider the entryway. What is there that gives these messages: "Welcome. Come in. Make yourself at home."
- Consider the registration area and reception area. Do parents feel they belong here? What signs tell you that other family members are welcome? Are there toys for children while their parents sign up or sign in? Is the area wheelchair accessible for family members who may need that accessibility? Is there evidence of what kind of program this is—child-centered decorations or products? Is the area aesthetic?
- Consider the furniture arrangements. In the office, is the visitor's chair across from the desk where the director or principal sits? Even such a simple device as moving the director's chair out from behind the desk and next to the visitor's chair changes a formal atmosphere to a warmer, friendlier one.
- How much of a natural environment is visible? Is there natural lighting, windows looking out at trees or plants? Is there an outdoor area for parents to make themselves comfortable?

26 FAMILY PARTICIPATION

RATIONALE

Sometimes called "parent involvement," family participation in preschool and infant-toddler programs includes anything from assisting in the classroom, to serving on a board or advisory committee, to building furniture. Other parent involvement activities can be: taking equipment home to repair, washing paint smocks, contributing supplies, or coming in on a Saturday to spruce up the yard. Attending parent education sessions is yet another example of family participation. Fund-raising is still another way that families can participate.

Cooperative preschools are one example of parent participation programs and are built on parent involvement. Traditionally they have focused more on the whole of development rather than the more narrow view of school readiness or academics. Many of the parent participation programs are sponsored by public school districts or linked with an adult education program. Often the parents run the program, hire the teacher, and/or sit on the decision-making board. Usually enrolled families are required to have a parent work in the classroom on a regular weekly basis. Sometimes the participating parents for that day meet after the session is over to discuss what happened. Usually the programs have children only half a day. These after-the-session meetings are part of the parent education arm of the program and are often coupled with night meetings for the whole group. Parents who have the time and interest in being deeply involved with their children's care and education are the ones who choose this type of program.

If the family's goal is child care while they work, or if they are sending the child to public school, required parent involvement may not be what the family wants or has time for. One of the themes of this book is to create partnerships with parents, so parent involvement that is mandated by the program can work against the partnership. If one program goal is empowerment, requiring families to do something they don't want to or don't have time for works in opposition to that goal. Anyone who is truly interested in developing partnerships with parents needs to think about how to use parent involvement toward that end rather than defeating it.

Joyce Epstein, director of the National Network of Partnership Schools, breaks parent involvement into six categories of activities used by schools:

1. Parent-education activities
2. Communications between schools and families
3. Volunteer opportunities
4. At-home learning activities
5. Decision-making opportunities
6. Community collaborations

Family participation and parent involvement have been around for a long time at all kinds of early childhood programs for children through age 8. One idea behind the concept is that success for the child is linked to families becoming part of their children's care and education program. Success may be defined as academic achievement, school readiness, enhanced learning, or optimal development of the whole child.

APPROACHES

- Start by making parents and other family members feel comfortable and welcome when they enter the program and then on a continuing basis.
- Set up an environment that says to family members, "You belong here." Include a place for them to sit, if possible, toys for younger siblings, and a bulletin board with items of interest for parents. Some programs have mailboxes for each family, pamphlets available, and even books to lend. A steaming coffee pot is an added bonus.
- An open-door policy lets families know that their presence is always welcome.
- Work to develop a relationship with each family member who comes into the program. Just being available when the child arrives or is picked up is a good beginning for a relationship.
- Find out what interests them and ask how the program can serve them better. When the family is a focus instead of just the child, programs can provide or organize activities that families really want to participate in, such as excursions, parties, and Friday night pizza and video for the whole family.
- Suggest ways they can help out or become part of the program. This works best after you get to know the family and understand their strengths, interests, and skills.
- Offering opportunities to observe can be a start for them to get to know the program and figure out where they best fit in as participating family members.
- Help each family to get to know other families in the program.
- If parents are willing to give out contact information, create an address list to pass out.
- Notice which children spend time with each other and tell the parents of both, in case they want to make play dates.
- Look for barriers that may be keeping some families from participating and see which ones you can eliminate. Can younger siblings come along with the parent who wants to spend time in the classroom? Can an occasional Saturday event help the parents who want to be involved, but are busy on weekdays?
- Recognize that some families see school as separate and apart from family life and expect the teachers to do the educating without involving them. The whole idea of parent involvement may be very strange, and parents may feel inadequate to see themselves as their "child's first teacher." Don't push them to do things they feel uncomfortable doing. Just keep working on building a relationship with them.

A story about family participation: One family felt so at home in their child care center that when the child went into kindergarten the family welcomed the list of ways to participate that the teacher

This cooperative preschool and kindergarten brochure states that the program is child-centered but the parents own the school, so there is a constant family presence in all aspects of its operation. The parent's role is spelled out in this brochure.

The School

Tucson Community School, Inc. ("TCS") is a non-profit, parent-owned cooperative for the children of Tucson. The school is governed by its Board of Directors, a group of current parents elected annually, and by its Board of Trustees.

TCS offers a three-year program that starts when a child is three years old by August 31st and continues through Kindergarten.

The school welcomes students of all races, religions, and cultures and maintains a financial assistance program that allows it to offer education to children of all economic levels. TCS is accredited by the National Association of the Education of Young Children (NAEYC) which provides goals and guidelines for quality education. Classroom visits and school tours are welcomed and encouraged. Please contact the office for an appointment with the Director.

History

As a parent cooperative, TCS was created, built, and maintained by dedicated mothers and fathers who wanted to actively participate in their child's education.

When founded in 1948, the school invited an educator from New York's prestigious Bank Street School to be its first director. Parents asked for her help in forming an innovative school. With the experience of more than 55 years, TCS has educated generations of young children.

Philosophy

The school maintains a consistent, child-centered program with developmentally-appropriate practices. The focus is learning through play both indoors and outdoors with an approach that promotes a positive self-concept.

TCS strives to be a safe place where children can learn to be creative, independent, problem-solving individuals. Its goal is to lay the foundation for the inner strength and resilience necessary for each child to meet the demands of his or her world.

The Child

Children are the focus of TCS. Teachers help each child feel capable and confident while stimulating his or her widening curiosity in a non-competitive environment. TCS believes it is the right of every child to be respected and treated as an individual. With mutual respect, children learn to share in group responsibility and develop self-discipline.

Children explore the world by working with natural materials, caring for animals and planting gardens. Creativity is developed through pretend play, music, painting, dancing, and block building. Understanding of numbers and words is incorporated in hands-on daily activities.

Large motor proficiency is acquired from biking, climbing, and running. Small motor skills are developed with puzzles, sewing and drawing. Interpersonal skills are built by children being encouraged to resolve conflicts themselves in a positive and constructive way and by making friendships with children of diverse backgrounds.

Activities are open-ended; children work at their own pace and learn in the manner in which they are best suited. Active play is balanced with quiet play; routines are balanced with new experiences.

The Parent's Role

As a parent cooperative, TCS relies on parents for many things. The commitment required of each family is significant; the benefits enjoyed by parents and children are far-reaching and long-lasting.

Each family agrees to be the helping parent in their child's classroom for one full morning a week for a period of 12 to 18 weeks. As a helping parent, the adult assists the teacher in various ways, including overseeing play, cleaning up activities, and preparing snacks. In this way parents are able to see their teacher and child in action.

In addition, each family is required to help at one maintenance work party per year, assist in the school's major fundraising event in the Fall and participate in their choice of school activities. These include the Spring Festival, Library Committee, and Make-a-plate, and can be selected according to parents' interest, abilities, and time.

Both at-home and working parents find that school participation is adaptable to their schedules. The school welcomes grandparents and babysitters as well.

Notes of appreciation are a good way to keep parents and other family members volunteering in the classroom.

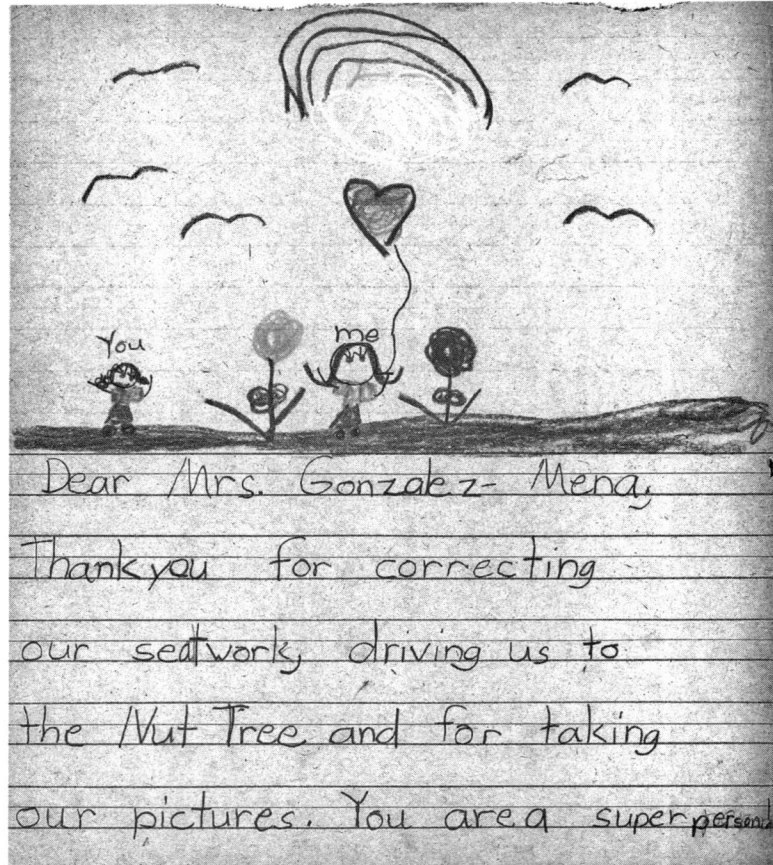

> Dear Mrs. Gonzalez-Mena,
> Thank you for correcting our seatwork, driving us to the Nut Tree and for taking our pictures. You are a super person!

Family participation and parent involvement have been around for a long time at all kinds of early childhood programs for children from birth through age 8. One idea behind the concept is that success for the child is linked to families becoming part of their children's care and education program.

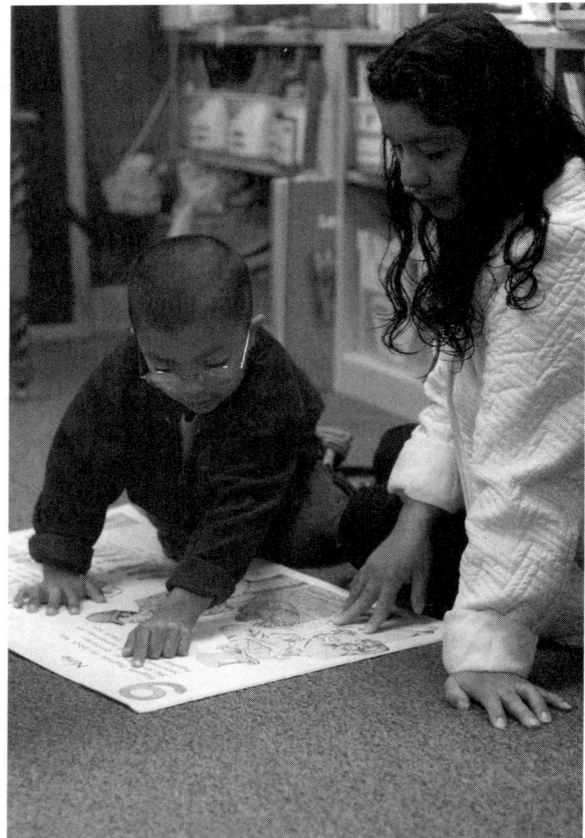

handed out the first day. This family became the catalyst for other families who weren't used to participating in their children's programs.

This family is a contrast to a family who came into the child care center with the idea that this was school and the teacher was the one who knows about education. They had great respect for this teacher—and any teacher—so they put her on a pedestal. Their attitude influenced their relationship with her. When this family met another family from their same culture who had a different idea about the child care center, they began to see a different perspective. The family they met had a cousin who was an assistant teacher in the program, and she helped them feel right at home in the center. Then they began to notice how involved their new friends were in the program and that gave them the idea that they could be involved too. Eventually they started looking for ways to help out. The grandmother one day offered to take home the paint smocks to wash over the weekend. On Monday when she brought the smocks back, she noticed a father reading a book in Spanish to a small group of children. That gave her the idea to offer to teach the children some songs and finger plays from her own childhood. Later the mother offered to come in and make tortillas with the children. While she was there, she got the idea that maybe the center could have a potluck evening when each family could bring an ethnic dish to share. What started as no involvement, ended up as plenty of involvement and none of it was required.

27 FAMILY SUPPORT SERVICES

▌RATIONALE

A leading voice in defining family support services comes from Ethel Seiderman, originator of the Parent Services Project, started in California in 1980 and by 2003 including 600 organizations representing 30,000 families in eight states. The principles of a family support program start with partnerships where the relationship between families and staff is one of equality and respect, resulting in a mutually beneficial partnership where power is shared. Families are seen as their own best advocates who can make decisions as part of a collaborative team. Families who are confident and competent empower their children to achieve success and well-being. Family strengths are a focus in family support programs. Seeking services is a sign of strength. Programs build on the strengths of families. Families are seen as assets, not barriers to overcome or work around. They are vital resources to themselves and to one another. Each family's culture is valued, recognized, and respected.

Programs are community based and are culturally and socially relevant to the families they serve. Family services are family driven. Families determine the program services that impact them. They make choices to participate in activities that reflect their own needs and interests. When appropriate,

Create, support, and maintain a partnership with families.

programs are a bridge between families and other services. Social support networks create connection and reduce isolation, promoting the well-being of the child, the family, and the community. Hope and joy are essential elements in building healthy communities. Families and staff in partnership create a context in which to nurture and experience hope and joy. Hope is connected to action, creating the energy and vitality to work for change.

APPROACHES

- Expand the focus from the child to the child and family.
- Create programs that build relationships with families based on equality and respect for each family within its cultural context.
- Create, support, and maintain a partnership with families.
- Make sure your image of families is as allies.
- Recognize that some families feel isolated and powerless. Create networks of social support to help them overcome those feelings.
- See families as resources for the program and for each other.
- Make family support a part of every aspect of your program.
- Help parents identify and find the services they need.
- Support parents in gaining the schools and tools they need.
- Be flexible and creative so you can respond to the strengths and needs of the particular group you serve.
- Become a community center. Some early care and education programs conceived themselves as community centers from the beginning. Others were designed to focus more narrowly on children with families peripheral to the operation. Public schools in many communities were orignally intended to be community centers. Some manage to continue to be community centers but others do to a lesser degree.

28   FATHERS: FOCUSING ON

RATIONALE

Fathers aren't all the same. Just as there are all kinds of mothers in all kinds of situations, the same is true for fathers. Some fathers live with the mother and their children and are closely connected; others live in the same house, but are not so closely connected. Some fathers live with the other father rather than a mother. In any family, there may be blood ties or not. There may be marriage ties or not. Some fathers live with their children as single parents. Some fathers are raising their stepchildren as single parents. It's very hard to make a generalized statement about fathers except to say that some ECE programs have a harder time involving men than they do women.

One group of fathers that may not get enough attention from ECE professionals are those who don't live with their children. Parent Services Project (mentioned in Strategy 15 about building communities) created a fatherhood project aimed at involving fathers who are not living with their children. A goal of the project was to give these fathers the support they needed to have positive relationships with their children. Some of them who never had affection in their own childhood learned to give it to their children, and they reaped the rewards of that behavioral change. The project put on workshops in parenting, which included communication and conflict resolution. The fathers also learned about stress management, as well receiving job training and learning financial management. The outcomes of that project were remarkable and included fewer child behavior problems, higher levels of sociability, and even a reduction in childhood poverty. Some of the fathers in this project turned their lives around, making changes that benefited themselves, their children, and their communities. As they got involved in early care and education programs, they learned the importance of making time for their children.

James Levine (1993) saw four barriers to getting men involved in Head Start and public preschool programs:

1. Father's fear of exposing inadequacies
2. Ambivalence of program staff members about father involvement
3. Gatekeeping by mothers
4. Inappropriate program design and delivery

When programs are designed for mother involvement rather than including both parents, men can feel uncomfortable and unwelcome. Some hints that this is happening comes when teachers tend to talk to the mothers, not the fathers; when conferences are held at times when few fathers can attend; when no men work in the program; and when a child lives in two homes but only one set of newsletters and notices are sent home.

Some men arrive in ECE programs already involved in their children's lives. They've had experience in PTA or other parent-teacher organizations as members or officers. Some have been involved with Little League as coaches. Many children enter kindergarten from Head Start where both their parents were involved. Those experienced fathers are sometimes more easily able to involve other fathers than are the teachers or staff in the program. If you can get them organized to reach out to other men, the rate of male involvement can go up.

To get men involved in most programs, the staff has to be intentional about it. Leaving male involvement to chance almost always means that more mothers will be involved than fathers. Stanley Seiderman, director of the Bay Area Male Involvement Network in California, had good ideas about how to make involvement in early care and education programs more attractive to men. He said, "The strongest motivators for getting and keeping fathers involved in all aspects of their child's life are expectation, encouragement and opportunity. While it is true that there are men who want to get involved and need little help to do so, most men will not usually come forward in our child care settings. They tend to be reticent and uncomfortable" (Lee, 2004).

APPROACHES

- Make all fathers feel welcome. Go back and look at Strategy 4 about creating an antibias environment. Read through each strategy, keeping a focus on fathers. Analyze an ECE environment in terms of fathers, keeping those strategies in mind. If you were a father, what would welcome you? What would feel less than inviting?
- Figure out how to get more male teachers and staff members. Explore the barriers to males entering the field and begin to address them. (See Strategy 2, Advocacy.)
- Recognize that males experience the world differently from the way females experience it. Though ECE professionals may have a strong value of gender equity, we still have to acknowledge that being a male is different from being a female. We might even see those differences in terms of cultural ones.
- Learn more about the differences in male and female experiences by observation and discussion. One way to learn more is to increase the number of male teachers and staff members, so the numbers are more even.
- Don't assume that what you know about the differences in male and female experiences are universal. Each culture varies in what males experience and what females experience. There is plenty to learn.
- Recognize that the field of early care and education has its own culture and those of us who have training and experience in the field have become part of it, though we may not even be aware of the idea of it being a culture. Female influences created this culture (consciously and unconsciously) more than male influences. This is a huge emotional subject and could be debated at length.
- Learn more about the ECE culture by observation and discussion. The more the ECE culture is talked about, the more aware we will all become of it.
- Look at little things that give messages to men about their place in the program. *Stronger Together* (Lee, 2004) suggests, for example, to look at the following:
  - Is the initial interview, if there is one, scheduled so both parents can attend?

Children benefit when their fathers are part of the early care and education program. Fathers benefit too!

○ Does the application form ask for the name, address, and phone number of the noncustodial parent or the mother's significant other?

○ Are men on the mailing list to receive all of the announcements, invitations, questionnaires, and bulletins?

○ Are parent-teacher conferences scheduled so both parents can come and are both expected?

○ Can men see and interact with other men in the classroom or at the center?

- Consider these ideas for getting men into the center, if hiring male teachers is difficult. Male bus drivers can double as classroom aides. High school and college students could volunteer as part of a class assignment. Community service clubs could send males to spend time with the children.

- Decide that men want to be involved and then proceed to include them in the decisions about *how* they want to be involved. Don't expect them to be automatically interested in everything that women teachers and mothers find engaging.

- Increase father involvement in your program by using some of these ideas:

○ Create activities especially for men. Ethel Seiderman's husband Stanley held Saturday morning breakfasts for fathers for many years at the child care center where Ethel was once director.

○ Hold an annual father's day picnic.

○ Have a father organize the other fathers for a workday in the center, classroom, or play yard. Mothers can be included, but if a father organizes it, men are more likely to come.

○ Research the best times to hold parent-teacher conferences so that fathers can come. Afternoons won't work for all fathers (or mothers either).

○ Have family parties where everybody is invited, including fathers and grandfathers too.

29

FIRST MEETING WITH FAMILIES

RATIONALE

Laying the foundation for the relationship starts when parents first meet the teacher, provider, director, or caregiver. The meeting is different depending on whether the family is choosing the program or family child care home from a number of available ones, glad to be accepted in the only program they qualify for, or going to their local neighborhood public school. The meeting may be set up for this one family or may be a group meeting with all the families who are enrolling their children. There are likely to be forms to fill out. If the family has the forms ahead of time, they can bring them to the meeting and discuss them there. This may be a time that the ECE professional gets to know something of the child's history in the family. It's important that the ECE professional explains how any information the parents give will be used.

Here is a fairly simple and straightforward form that supplies basic information about the family and the child and invites the family members to volunteer in the classroom. It also gives the option of doing work at home for the class. Notice that the form asks for "parent(s) name(s)," which makes it appropriate for single-parent families, and also for families with parents of the same sex.

Home/School Connection

Child's Name_____ Birthday _____

Parent(s) Name(s) _____

Siblings (names and ages)_____

_____

Address _____

Home Phone # _____ Work Phone # _____

Pets (kind/name) _____

Hobbies/Interests _____

_____

Name you want your child to learn to write:

First:_____ Last:_____

Some things you may want to know about my child: (use back if necessary)

_____

_____

_____

Are you interested in volunteering in the classroom?_____
Times of Availability: M_____ T_____ W_____ T_____ F_____

Are you interested in doing work at home?_____

Programs for children age 5 and under sometimes have a parent handbook that contains information the parents need. The table of contents of this parent handbook from a developmental children's center shows that it is full of specifics that many families will appreciate having in writing.

TABLE OF CONTENTS

In some programs the first encounter with the parents involves dealing with a good deal of paperwork, including forms related to the family income level and other forms to be signed, acknowledging that the staff is required to report any suspected child abuse. That makes an unfortunate beginning if the emphasis is to be on human relationships.

When parents and professionals can just talk together and share information, they are off to a better start. Of course, it is useful to have parents fill out a form that lets them explain their child's particular needs, ways of expressing herself, and other important information. Parents are also usually grateful for written information about the program, although they may prefer to take it home to read it. If the meeting is designed to be comfortable, relaxing, and not overwhelming, it's a better start. Additionally, when the meeting is set up for each family separately, it's a good chance to begin a relationship.

APPROACHES

- Find out right away what the family members want to be called and what they want you to call their child. Tell them what you want to be called. Be aware of cultural differences in use of names and titles. If you prefer to be called by your first name, some families may feel uncomfortable calling you that, and even more uncomfortable letting their child call you that. Some families may want their child to call you "teacher" without using your name, which may feel uncomfortable to you, but for them is an appropriate sign of respect for your position.

Although it is important to prepare parents for the separation difficulties their children might have when they first start in a program, this family obviously didn't need much preparation. This child is happy to say good-bye!

- Discuss possible separation issues the child might have as he or she starts the program. Share ideas with the parents and listen to theirs about how to help their child cope with feelings about separation.
- For the youngest children, having the first meeting in their own home allows them to meet the new adult in their life on their own home turf. In most cases, that is difficult, but when it works out, there are a number of benefits for both child and the family.
- If possible, invite the child and a family member to visit the program before actually starting in it. This pre-entry visit can ease the parents' minds as they watch the teacher interact with the child and see how things work in the program.
- If all the children are starting at the same time, staggering their entry can help them get more adult attention than if the whole group arrives the first day at the same time.
- Ideally the first days should be short ones. That is not always possible, but it is worth aiming for.
- Although some programs have a policy about parents not staying in the classroom while their children are first adjusting, there are advantages to having a different policy. When parents ease their children into a program and are there for them at first, it not only sets a tone of welcome for the parents and their involvement, but makes an easier transition for the child. (See Strategy 45 on transition into a program.)
- Recognize that it's quite natural for some parents to have strong feelings about being separated from their children. Empathize with those parents and avoid judging them as too attached or overprotective. Parent emotions can be complicated and intense. They may experience feelings of ambivalence about leaving their children, worries about safety and the quality of care, and fears about their child becoming attached to someone else. (See Strategy 17 on competition.)
- For those parents who have never separated from the children until this point, it may be helpful for them to know about the kinds of behaviors that are common in children. When this subject is

discussed openly, it can relieve parents' minds that the ECE professional isn't judging them or their child. Separation behaviors in young children can include:

○ Crying, clinging, protesting
○ Increased dependence
○ Difficulty in eating
○ Fears about going to sleep
○ Regressive behaviors—going back to an earlier stage in their lives—such as wetting their pants, thumb sucking
○ Passive behavior—as if they aren't quite "there"

30 HOME VISITS

RATIONALE

Some early childhood programs are conducted entirely in the home by home visitors. Often these programs are staffed by paraprofessionals who are trained and supervised by someone who is a qualified early childhood educator. The goals of these programs may vary depending on what groups are targeted for home visits—they may be families of children with special needs, or low-income families, whose children are thought to be at risk for school failure. In any case, the goals are usually to help families stimulate the learning and development of their children. Some are clear about the goal of turning the parents into teachers of their children. Some home visitors focus on helping parents see the opportunities for learning in everyday caregiving routines and household events. Others bring toys, equipment, and activities into the home for the children and parents to play with together. The home visitor may work with the child with the idea of modeling for the parents. Or the home visitor may sit back and encourage the parent to interact with the child.

There are advantages to using paraprofessionals as home visitors besides the cost factor. The home visitor who is of the culture and language background of the family is bound to have an easier time communicating and establishing rapport. Furthermore, the home visitor may be a member of the community and can serve as a resource to the parent. Some programs have more of a social work function than others who focus strictly on education. Home visitors can be greatly appreciated by families who feel isolated and see how the home visitor can help them interact in more effective and positive ways. Home visitors can sometimes help families make great improvements in their lives, especially when a trusting relationship is established.

A different type of home visit is when ECE professionals who work in center-based settings or schools come once or periodically visit the child in his or her own home. Why do home visits? Home visits are not a universal aspect of early care and education programs for several reasons. They are hard to schedule. ECE professionals already have enough to do and may see home visits as just one thing too many. Parents may feel threatened by an outsider coming into their home. Even though there are reasons *not* to make home visits a part of the ECE program, still, those who do home visits often swear by the benefits and see them as outweighing the problems. Seeing a child in the context of home and family can be extremely valuable. Furthermore, by making a visit to the home, teachers show that they care enough to go beyond the school or center walls. Some reasons for doing home visits are that you can do the following:

- Meet family members who never come to the center or school.
- Get to know the child better and have a better understanding of who he or she is and the background of the child's family life.
- Find out more about the child's interests, skills, and learning styles in a different context from the center or classroom.
- Learn more about the family and the resources they may have to offer your program.
- Solidify the relationship with the family by meeting them on their own territory.
- See how the family members and the child interact at home.
- Complement what the parents are doing at home.

Although home visits are more
common in preschool programs,
this form is from a first-grade
teacher who sends it home when
parents indicate that they would
like a visit.

Bring Home Your Teacher

School is a crowded place. Sometimes it feels like there is very little
time to spend with individual students, getting to know who they are on
their own and away from school. Also many first grade students are
amazed to learn that their teacher does not sleep on the couch in the
classroom, but is a real person outside school, too.

A strong home-school connection can make school a more effective
teaching and learning environment and a warmer, friendlier place.
Sometimes a home visit can help children feel more comfortable with their
teacher and the school setting.

**If you would like to have your teacher pay a short visit to
your house, please fill out the bottom of this form and return to
school.** I'll try to accomodate all requests as soon as possible. If this is not
a convenient time for a visit, feel free to request a visit later in the year at a
more convenient time. Also, if you are not comfortable with a visit in your
home, perhaps you'd like to have a visit at a park or another place away
from home that is more to your liking. The important part is a pleasant time
together socializing away from school. **No special preparation on your
part is necessary.**

Your teacher,

Ms. Kitty Ritz

• •

Child's name _____

___ Yes, I'd like to have a teacher visit

___ at my home   ___ at _____
                                        location

on _____
          day of the week

at _____.
          time of day

_____ No, thanks, but maybe another time.

Home visits give teachers a
chance to meet family members
who never come to the center or
school. They also provide
opportunities for the teacher to
get to know the child in a
different context.

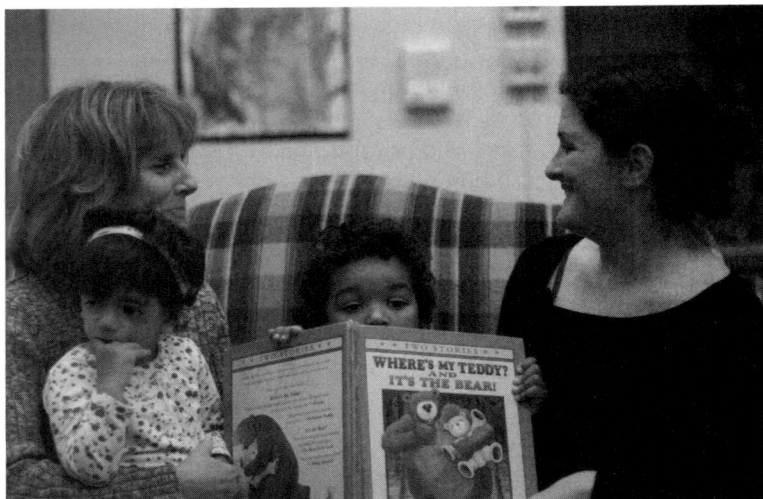

APPROACHES

- Don't judge. Parents may worry that the reason for the home visit is to judge the way they live or the way they are raising their children. They may have had experiences with other professionals coming into their home to monitor them, and they may associate this other experience with the teacher coming to visit.
- Be clear about the purpose of your home visit and explain in advance so the families know the reason. This information should be conveyed in the parent orientation and in the handbook as well. Try to reduce any threatening aspects of the home visit.
- Make arrangements in advance and follow up with a reminder just before the visit. Never surprise families.
- Recognize that you are entering the family's territory and put on your best guest manners. Be polite and sensitive. A follow-up thank-you note is a nice touch.
- Be aware that cultural differences may show up during a home visit. Be prepared to be flexible. For example, even if you are not hungry, it may be rude to refuse a family's offering of food.
- Dress appropriately—in a way that makes the family comfortable instead of uncomfortable. This takes sensitivity.
- Be on time and don't stay too long.
- Afterwards, reflect on how the home visit went and if it served a useful purpose.

31 IMMIGRANT FAMILIES

RATIONALE

Newly arrived immigrant families have a good many challenges. A huge one is language. At a time when they have so many new things to learn, their communication system is compromised. All the change of leaving the old behind and starting new in a strange culture brings stress. Language difficulties greatly add to the stress. Nothing is easy, and they meet up with intolerant people while they are getting settled—finding a place to live, signing up for utilities, understanding the transportation system, and getting a new job. When people can't understand them, they get impatient with the immigrants. In a new language and culture they are slower than in their old country. They make many mistakes and sometimes are regarded as ignorant; however, if you could see them operate in their own language and familiar surroundings, they aren't the same people!

At a time when they need support, many immigrants are on their own. They have had to leave their support networks behind, including the extended family. Maybe for the first time in their lives they are alone in the world.

After immigrants have been here awhile, the children in the family often get ahead of the adults in learning the language and figuring out new ways of the society they live in. That situation puts parents at a huge disadvantage because traditional roles are reversed. Now the children are the ones who know best. They may even be embarrassed by their parent's awkward ways and difficulties in communication, even their accents. Where once respect for the authority of elders was the rule, now it is the children who are the authorities. What worries for a family! Discipline may no longer work and the children, too, are on their own.

Even though families may be uncomfortable about what is happening to their children, they often are forced to put them in out-of-home care. Grandma is no longer there to stay with them. They have mixed feelings about turning their children over to nonfamily members. They may worry about identity issues and the fact that their children may become assimilated and lose their cultural ties.

Although sometimes immigrant families disagree with what they see in the early care and education program, they feel as if they are putting their children into the hands of those they consider to be the authority, especially if such a person is called teacher or director. "The professional knows best" is their attitude. They have great respect for authority. Some families still see themselves as the authority at home; in their minds they create a huge separation between what they do at home and what happens in the early childhood program. Other families grant the ECE professional supreme authority over all things to do with children, both in the program and at home. They see their job is to learn about it so they can do the same at home. One young teacher told a family recently immigrated from another country that they should speak English to their children at home. They followed her advice even though their ability to speak English was limited. The result was that parent-child communication was greatly limited and everyone was frustrated for a long time. The parents' English improved, but they always had a heavy accent and never became truly articulate in that language as compared to their own. The children learned English from school and from their peers, but lost their home language to their parents' great sorrow.

Alicia Lieberman, a mental health specialist, offers strategies for working with immigrant families in her article, "Concerns of Immigrant Families" (1995). The strategies she suggests include the following:

This sign was on the wall of a kindergarten classroom to make families feel welcome when they found their own language displayed.

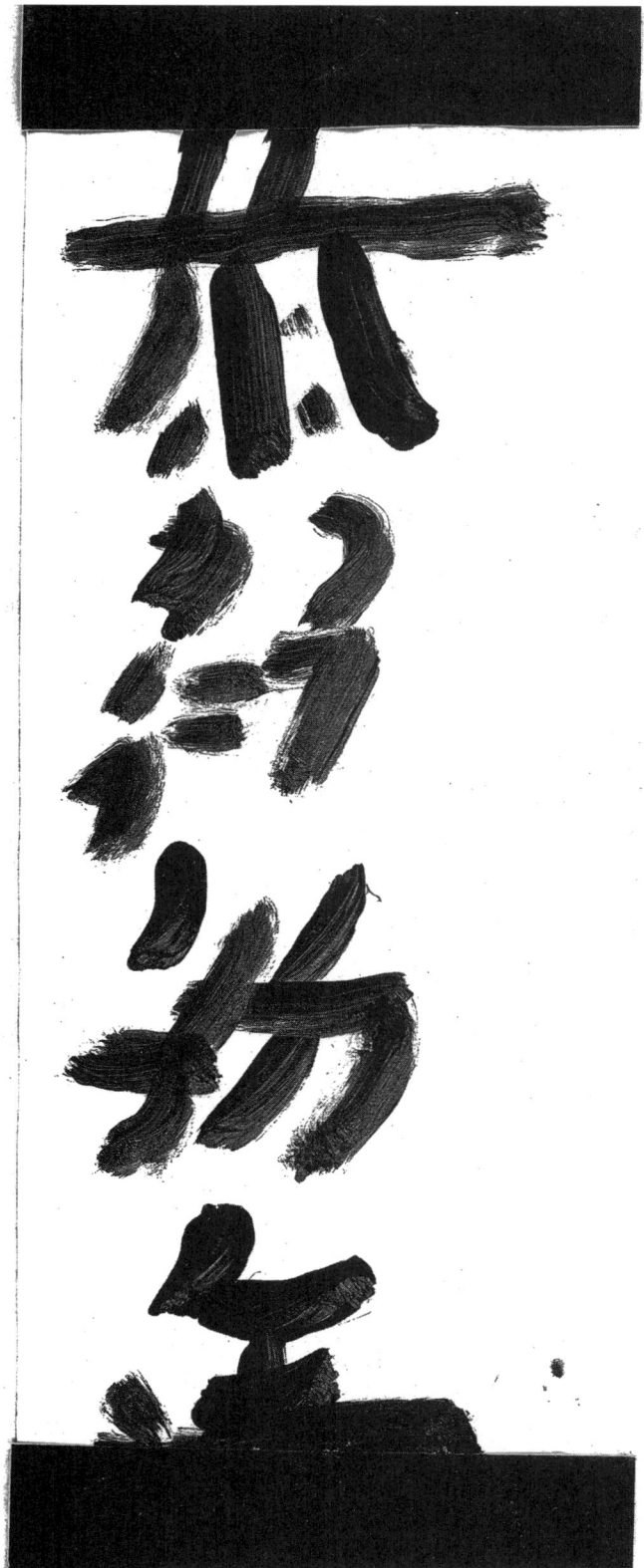

APPROACHES

- Remember the language difference. Talk as clearly as you can in short sentences and plain words.
- Explain the routine of the program or classroom. The families may come from countries where the customs are very different.
- Acknowledge tension and think about the reasons for it. The chances are that the tension between you and the parent is due to cultural differences.
- Ask parents about their child-rearing practices. Find out how things are done in their country when you don't understand a particular behavior or practice. Try to communicate about your differences so that it's just that—a difference—and not a deficiency.
- Serve as a cultural bridge between the parents' culture and the culture of child care. Help them understand the way things are done in the center or classroom.
- Remember that you are an authority figure and most families want your approval.
- Establish a trusting atmosphere that encourages dialogue. Build trust before you try discussing problems and when you do, try to discuss them in ways that avoid a critical tone and instead express care and concern.
- Remember that immigration causes great stress for the whole family. The people who felt self-confident and competent in their home country now are trying learn some basic skills. They may be suffering from depression. But many immigrants with children in early care and education programs are full of hope for the future. You are part of that hope.
- Appreciate their culture, support them, and help them adjust to life in a new country.

Notice what is on the bulletin board under Broadway Children's School. How do you think immigrants feel when they find their own language in evidence around the classroom? That's one way of saying, "You are welcome here."

32 INCLUSION OF FAMILIES OF CHILDREN WITH SPECIAL NEEDS

RATIONALE

Classrooms and centers set up for typically developing children are now required by law to accept children with special needs. All children must be provided with care and education in the least restrictive setting where their typically developing peers are served. That law has provided benefits to everybody—not just children and families with special needs. By making a program or school inclusive everybody gains for the following reasons:

1. Diversity of all sorts is a bonus. Everybody benefits from being around people who are different from themselves—children and parents alike—especially if the early childhood professionals know how to help them appreciate differences and interact with each other in respectful ways.

2. Children with special needs benefit by being integrated with their typically developing peers instead of segregated into special education programs. They learn to live in a world that has a greater variety of people in it than they find in special education programs that are exclusively for them.

3. Teachers benefit by expanding their knowledge of how to meet a variety of needs, some of which they might not have encountered before they experienced inclusion.

4. Families who have children with special needs benefit from being integrated with families who have typically developing children and learning about them and their successes and challenges, just as those families benefit from learning about the successes and challenges of families of children with special needs.

APPROACHES

- If parents of children who have special challenges or disabilities do not arrive in the classroom already as advocates for their children, encourage them to take on that role. (See Strategies 1 and 2 on advocacy.) They will need those skills as their children move on from your program or classroom to others. If they are already advocates, you need to appreciate that. You can learn a good deal from families and from the specialists with whom they are involved.
- Give emotional support to all families when needed. Recognize that families who have children with special needs or challenges may need even more support and understanding. Although many families have already had plenty of experience of coping with their emotions, others may be still in the stages of grieving that accompany the discovery that their child's development is not typical. Feelings of anger, sadness, resentment, frustration, and guilt are common.
- Don't judge parents who are in denial or seem to you to be overprotective of their child. Accept them as they are and realize that these are common responses for parents in their situation.
- Understand that some families have had multiple experiences working with professional experts and their reactions to you may have nothing to do with you personally. If their experiences with other experts have been negative, it may take more time to build a relationship with these parents than with parents who enter the program with little or no prior experience with experts.
- Be prepared to connect with specialists (if any) who are working with the family. Teamwork is important in meeting any child's needs, and the team may be expanded when meeting the special

needs of some children. Parents may know more about their child's condition than you do, and the specialists working with them may have expertise that you can use.

- Use "people first" terminology. Don't say "a disabled child"; say "a child with a disability." Don't say "special-needs family"; say "a family that has a child with special needs."
- Provide opportunities for the both child and the family members to integrate into the program or classroom. Introduce the family to other families and help them to get to know each other.
- Learn about community resources (see Strategy 16) that are available to all families. The family who has a child with a disability or other challenges may be able to expand your knowledge of community resources based on their experience.
- The other strategies in this book that apply to parents in general can be used to work equally well with parents of children with special needs.

A story about the benefits of parent involvement in an inclusion program: A mother brought her baby to a Mommy and Me class for the first time when he was 17 months old. Her child was born with a heart defect and had several surgeries in his young life. His main experience outside the home was with heart specialists and medical procedures. The nursery classroom was an entirely new experience for both him and his mother. His mother was shocked when she saw the skills that other children her son's age had developed. It was her first experience being around babies other than her own, and she had no idea of the developmental issues her child had been dealing with—issues that had been ignored in the interest of saving his life. She vowed from that day forward to start focusing more on his development and less on his medical problems, and she spoke right away to the specialists who had been seeing her son. They directed her to the resources she needed. She continued in the class, and everybody was delighted at the progress the boy made in a short time, once he got in an environment that was developmentally appropriate and conducive to his needs.

33 MEETINGS

RATIONALE

All types of meetings for parents can occur in early care and education programs. Several types are discussed in Strategies 18, 19, and 44 on conferences. Also the first meeting with families gets special consideration in Strategy 29. That's another specific kind of meeting. This chapter is about meetings in general, which can include parent discussion groups, informal support groups, planning meetings for fund-raising, planning meetings for field trips, board or counsel meetings, reading and study groups, and any other kind of meeting you can think of. Sometimes parents get together regularly to do crafts and talk.

Meetings are more effective if they are planned around what families think they need rather than what teachers think the families need. When parents and other family members have a chance to express what they want and share their interests, they may be more inclined to attend meetings. It's best if families choose and guide the agenda of meetings.

If some of the meetings are designed as "parent education," be sure that the format is an interactive one rather than the delivery of information from some expert. Although lectures may be interesting to some parents, that format fails to acknowledge that those in the audience have expertise as well. Delivering information in ways that ignore the competencies of the parents leads the relationship between staff and families away from partnerships. Strategy 35 discusses parent education further.

APPROACHES

- Plan group size and style of the meeting so it meets the parents' needs for comfort and provides an opportunity to talk to each other. Small groups create feelings of closeness, community, and ownership of the meeting. Meetings of one classroom or center are more effective than whole school meetings.
- Select a good time for the meeting. Get family input about the best date and time. Some parents find it enticing to come after work and have supper provided, followed by the meeting. Other parents who work close by can do "brown-bag" meetings at lunchtime.
- Provide child care, if needed.
- Be clear about the purpose of the meeting.
- Consider involving the children in making invitations to or refreshments for the meeting. They can also provide decorations.
- Try to create a warm, friendly atmosphere where people feel like sharing.
- Use name tags if the parents don't know each other.
- Use icebreakers to help get participants acquainted with each other. Some kind of active exercise can help participants feel comfortable and relaxed. It creates a conducive atmosphere for interaction and sets a tone for the meeting.
- Plan meetings to encourage interaction among the participants. Discussion works better than lectures.
- Bring in interpreters, if needed, so everyone understands everything.
- Consider your role in the meeting. If you can be a facilitator, rather than the person in charge, it's more likely that participants will interact with each other. As a facilitator your role can be to provide some structure and ensure that everybody gets to talk.

Two versions of an open house invitation—one in English and one in Spanish.

Date _____

Dear _____,

    I really want you to come to see _____

_____

in Room 28. Please come Tuesday, _____ from 7:45 to 8:15 a.m.

    Love,

_____

Estimada/o _____

Deseo que Ud. venga al "Open House" en el aula No. 28.

La clase estará abierta de las _____ a las _____.

Me gustaría mostrarle _____

Pienso que le gustaría ver _____

Una cosa que le quisiera leer es _____

_____

- Don't think you have to be the only one planning and facilitating meetings. Let the families create a committee that takes over that job. Or share the responsibility with them.

  Icebreakers for parent meetings:

  ○ Name Game. Use a light-weight ball or a soft throwable object for this icebreaker. Say the name of a participant and toss him or her the ball. Tell that participant to do the same until all the participants have been named aloud.
  ○ Pair up participants with people they don't know and give them a few minutes to get acquainted with their partner. Have them introduce each other to the group.

34 PARENT COMPLAINTS: WORKING WITH

RATIONALE

One parent is always in the director's office with a new criticism or complaint. She used to talk to the teachers but they got tired of it, so they started making sure that when she is around they are too busy to listen. Now she goes to the director. This is not an uncommon situation. Why all these complaints?

Only when you understand what's going on with this parent can you determine what to do about it. It helps to think about how parents, usually mothers, are responsible for the well-being of their young children, which includes even the most personal aspects of their daily care. When all of that is out of the parents' hands, they may feel frustrated that they can't control or to some extent even know how it is being done. This can weigh heavily on parents to have the responsibility and not be in charge because they have to delegate it.

Lynet Uttal (2002) made an ethnographic study of mothers who had children in child care arrangements and among other things found that the responsibility for choosing care and education programs for their children was left up to mothers, even if fathers or other family members were part of the picture. With responsibility comes the potential for error. The mothers wanted very much to believe that their children were getting high-quality care, but they were worried a good deal that perhaps they had made a bad choice and their children were not in the best situation. They exhibited ambivalence in most cases, and it centered on how to monitor and ensure the quality of their arrangements. Worries about safety were high on the list. Programming and staffing were also concerns. They were constantly wondering about things like what was the relationship like between their child and the professional? What kind of care was their child getting anyway? What if their child cried and nobody paid attention? What was that bruise on the child's leg? How was the child being disciplined? Or was there no discipline? Those questions weighed heavily on the minds of women she interviewed.

Of course, every article in the paper about suspected abuse in a family child care home or center intensifies all the worries. Who is watching out for the children is a question parents have to ask when their children are in homes and institutions where they can't monitor them very well.

In Uttal's study, how comfortable mothers were about their children's out-of-home experience depended on the relationships they had with their children's care and education professionals. Uttal made it clear that relationships really matter!

The mother in the opening of this chapter doesn't seem to have much of a relationship with the staff. It's easy to say it is her own fault, but is it? Whose responsibility is it to build the relationship? In a world where parents may feel like guests at best and intruders or spies at worst in their children's care and education settings, it is up to the professionals to help them feel otherwise by working on building a relationship with each one.

So let's look back at the mother who always criticizes and complains. Maybe behind the complaints are worries and frustrations. Maybe she has ambivalent feelings about her child being in care at all. Maybe she feels guilty. Are her criticisms and complaints a way of making her feel like she is taking charge? Fulfilling her responsibilities? Maybe this parent is feeling like the care of her child is out of her hands and she wants to have more involvement in it. She doesn't know how to get involved except to be critical of what is going on. In that case, give her more options to be part of things.

A completely different explanation might be that maybe this parent feels she doesn't get enough attention. Maybe the only way that anybody listens to her is when she complains. She's like the child who is ignored until he misbehaves. You can't just keep ignoring the child, or the parent. They need attention, and they are getting it in a way that works. You have to show them that other ways work too.

Give her recognition when she is not complaining. It may not be easy, but just as we can work with children by giving them the attention they need at appropriate times, we can do the same with adults.

APPROACHES

- Try to understand what it must be like to be in this mother's position.
- Work on building a relationship with her by initiating contact instead of sending her away when she initiates it. Get to know her. Find a way to spend some time with her when you're not so busy with the children. If you begin to relate to one another, her complaining may ease up.
- Take her seriously and try to make her feel at home in the program.
- Try to get her involved in helping out.
- Introduce her to some other parents.
- Discuss with the director what else can be done.
- Get other staff members involved.

35

PARENT EDUCATION:
A TRANSFORMATIVE APPROACH

RATIONALE

Many people think of education involving a teacher and a learner having separate roles. The teacher teaches and the learner learns. In early childhood programs this idea can apply to children and also to parents when the program where their children go has a parent education component. In this particular model the learner is the parent and the teacher is the early childhood professional or some other expert. This view of education is based on the idea that the teacher has a body of knowledge and a set of skills; the goal, therefore, is to transmit the knowledge and skills to the learner.

A different model involves a two-way process in which the roles of teacher and learner are more fluid and dynamic. This model looks at teacher and learner sharing roles. In this model teachers are most effective when they also see themselves as learners. They get to know their students, who they are, what they are interested in, what they know and can do, what they need to know and be able to do, and how best they can learn. Teachers also learn, mostly by observing, where the learning edge of each student lies. Lev Vygotsky, a Russian theorist, used the term the Zone of

Parent education comes in many different forms. It becomes transformative when the teacher and learner share information in such a way that both learn something.

Proximal Development (ZPD) for the student's learning edge, that is, what each student is ready to learn next.

Using these ideas of teacher as learner and student as teacher, it is possible to move away from parent education that is based on a knowledge transmission model and move toward what is called a transformative education model. In simple terms, transformative education is when two people or groups come together and through their interactions both are changed for the better. Transformative education as it relates to parent education assumes that both teacher and family have bodies of knowledge that complement each other. Transformative education is vital when diversity is present. Diversity is always present, even among groups of people who look like they are from the same race and culture. Dig a little deeper and you find generational, religious, economic, gender, age, and ability differences, just for starters.

Transformative education doesn't preclude holding workshops or creating classes in parenting or offering books and other resources for the parents' edification. It just means that the teacher realizes that there are a variety of perspectives on everything relating to child care and education. He is sensitive to differences and seeks to understand them. It's a matter of openness rather than persuasive salesmanship. Teachers can gain a great deal of knowledge themselves through a transformative education process.

Looking at a situation where obvious diversity is present, imagine an immigrant family who is new to an early care and education program. When the early childhood professional is using a transformative education model, she doesn't just set out to teach them child development or how to improve their child's academics, but she works to learn what she can about who they are and what they want for their child. She explains (through a translator, if necessary) how the program works, and she also asks about their expectations. She asks if there are early care and education programs in their country and how it is the same or different from here. Her motive is to try to discover where there's a fit and what might cause them discomfort in this program. She doesn't do this all at once, but slowly over time, while working on the relationship. Both parties—the family and the teacher—gain from their many conversations and they get to know each other as well. Trust builds.

It may seem like a luxury to have so many conversations with a family. See Strategy 21 for ideas on how to find and create opportunities to talk to families.

APPROACHES

- Work on building a relationship with each family. Get to know them.
- Establish from the first day you meet the family and their child that you want to learn about them, including what their dreams are for their child and their ideas about how to fulfill them.
  - CAUTION: Be careful to go slowly. Mention your goal, but before going further, read their response. Are they suspicious, insecure, or hesitant to reply? Some families have many experiences of being questioned by authorities who have control over their lives. You want to develop a different kind of relationship, so be careful not to ask too many questions or leave them feeling like they have been interrogated.

- Keep an open mind. If a family tells you they want something that you disagree with, suspend judgment until you are sure you understand them. In the face of cultural or economic differences, misunderstandings are easy.
- Don't just ask questions, but observe as well and comment on what you see. Sometimes asking questions doesn't work as well as just remarking about what strikes you.
- Encourage the family to observe in the program if they have time and are comfortable doing so. Ask them to comment on what they see and listen to them with an open mind.
- Become aware of your stereotypes and put them aside along with your judgments. Make your goal to get to know this family uncluttered by stereotypic images.
- Notice when something a family member says or does causes discomfort in you. Being aware of your own reactions gives you some clues about what you need to learn more about.

- Besides your daily work and the interactions with each family, put together a more formal parent education program, which can include the following:
  - ○ Special meetings with a topic that parents agree is one they want to know more about. Be sure to have translators for families who need them.
  - ○ Discussion groups about issues that come up in which parents have an interest.
  - ○ Home visits if parents are comfortable with the idea.
  - ○ Opportunities for observation and discussion with you.
  - ○ A resource area with information the parents can use.

36 PARENTS IN THE CENTER OR CLASSROOM

RATIONALE

A common way of involving family members in their children's education is to invite them to volunteer in the classroom. Head Start has used this strategy successfully since it started in the mid-sixties. Other preschool and infant-toddler programs also utilize parent volunteers, but not all of them. For some programs it is mandated; for others not. Parent participation programs depend on parents as teachers to fill out ratios. Whether kindergarten and primary teachers use parent volunteers depends on many factors, including district policies and regulations, specialized funding, school traditions, and the teachers' own inclinations.

Having parents in the center or classroom works well when ECE professionals are dedicated to families and view their job as family-centered care and education. It doesn't work as well when ECE professionals come into the field because they like working with children, but dislike working with parents. In some cases, this is an early stage of professional development—the focus on the children and disregard of parents—but in other cases, this attitude remains throughout the career of the professional.

Certainly family members in the center or classroom complicate the job of the professional. For one thing it increases the number of people and interactions. The teacher, staff, or caregiver must plan for the extra adults as well as for the children. Children can behave very differently in the presence of their parents, which can disrupt the group.

Advocates for parents in the center or classroom cite many advantages. Family members who spend time being involved in their children's education learn about what goes on in the classroom and see how their children learn. Many parents' experience as an early learner occurred in a more highly structured, strict, academic environment and it helps them to understand developmental processes and the special approaches that work for children in their beginning years. Family members in the classroom can observe firsthand the ways their children interact with others. It broadens their view of their own children. For some parents being involved in the classroom is an eye-opening experience as they learn more about typical development.

Volunteering in the center or classroom makes parents and other family members feel good to be able to contribute to the program. The more time they spend there, the more ideas they come up with about how they can use their own talents, skills, and interests to make unique contributions. When they see how other parents bring in cultural artifacts and activities, that idea spreads.

Feelings of security on the part of the parents and their children increase when parents spend time in the classroom or center. The relationships between families and staff can solidify as they get to know each other better than just the quick daily hellos and good-byes and scattered meetings throughout the year.

APPROACHES

- Consider instituting an "open-door" policy that encourages parents and other family members to feel free to visit the center or classroom at any time. Or for some professionals a more specific visiting time may work better—such as one afternoon a week, family members are invited to come early and visit before their children go home.

Parent volunteers come into the classroom to take dictation as children learn that what they say can be represented in written words. This was an October activity and represents a story by Timmy about a pumpkin. Later he copied the story himself on another piece of paper.

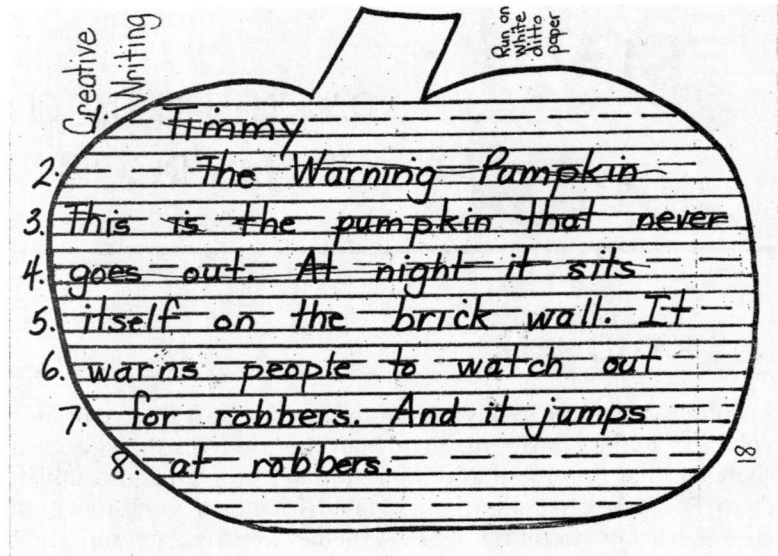

Creative Writing

Run on white ditto paper

1. Timmy
2. The Warning Pumpkin
3. This is the pumpkin that never
4. goes out. At night it sits
5. itself on the brick wall. It
6. warns people to watch out
7. for robbers. And it jumps
8. at robbers.

Preschoolers get more personal attention when parent volunteers are in the center encouraging the children to get involved in the various activities set out for them. A parent volunteer helped with this art project.

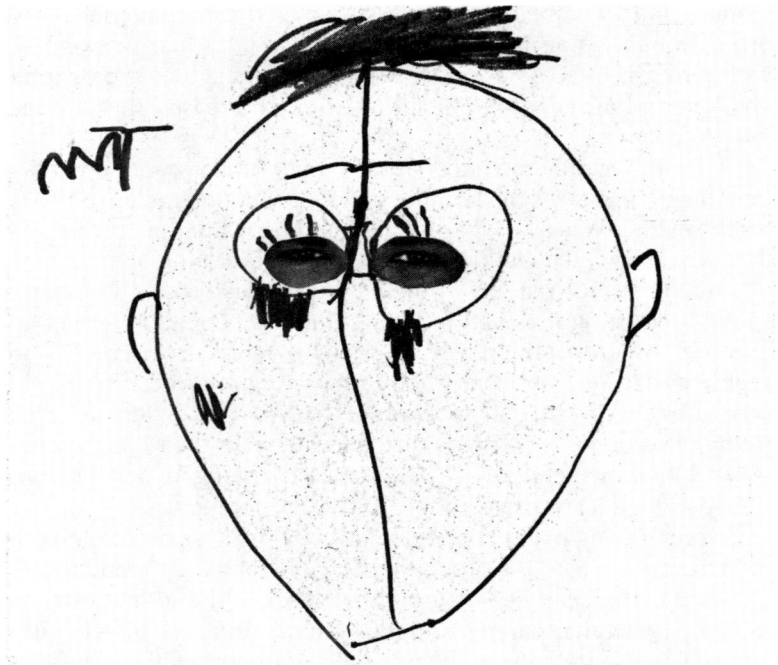

- If parents and other family members are coming into the classroom to assist the teacher or caregiver, it makes them feel more secure if there is some kind of training they can receive—either formal or informal.
- Informal training takes into consideration what beginners need to know right away. Certainly they need to know the expectations of the professional and the routine of the classroom. They need a description of what they are to do and instructions or tips about how to do it. Some of these things they can learn over time, but they need definite instructions for their first day. A day of observation before they begin to actually help out can give them an idea of how things work.

A common way of involving family members in their children's education is to invite them to volunteer in the classroom.

- A formal training program could include the specifics included under informal training, plus a broader overview of the field, such as an orientation to the principles, practices, and goals that relate to early childhood philosophy. Developmental information can be useful as well, plus some ideas about learning styles and how to respond to individual children as well as groups. Some tips on guidance approaches will help the parents understand what the professional is doing and make them feel more secure when they are faced with the need to guide behavior into positive routes.

- Invite parents to observe. This is a very different role from helping out and needs to be explained to everybody—children and parents. It helps if there is a special badge to wear or a certain chair to sit in or some other way of signaling that the family member is in an observation mode so that everybody understands what to expect.

- Consider other possibilities of parents in the center or classroom besides using them as helpers or assistant teachers or observers. They can help plan and carry out special social events for special occasions or for birthdays. Be sure before instituting this idea, though, that all families are okay with celebrations. Some families, for religious reasons, cannot participate in such events. Be sensitive to differences and honor them. A different way of bringing parents into the classroom is what one first-grade teacher does. She has parents come in twice a week for half an hour the first thing in the morning to read to and with their children. Many of those who show up are fathers.

37

PARTNERSHIPS: BUILDING THEM WITH FAMILIES

RATIONALE

Partnerships with families are not a given in early care and education programs. Indeed, if you explore the images of the relationship between ECE professionals and families, you may find a great variety of them. Expert/amateur, professional/client, and server/served are some images (perhaps unconscious) that lie in the heads of professionals. True partnerships don't fit into any of those images. Partnerships require two-way interactions and commitment. They don't come from the top down.

The partners don't have to be alike; they don't have to have the same skills. In fact, partnerships work better when the partners have different strengths—strengths that complement each other. One thing both sides need is to have a sense of power in the relationship.

If a partnership is to exist, it is the teacher, caregiver, or director's job to initiate it. So in some ways, unless mandated, the partnership depends on the professional to make it happen. Let's examine what it takes in the professional to create and support partnerships:

1. A strong sense of a particular kind of professionalism. The usual image of a professional is a bit cold and distant. Business clothes may be part of the image. Most early childhood professionals don't fit that image and they can't if they are to be partners with parents. They need to create relationships and that means they can't be cold and distant, but must be warm and personable.

2. Self-respect and respect for others are two key ingredients of a professional/family partnership.

3. Clarity about the importance of building partnerships and a commitment to do so.

4. Sensitive, self-reflective, and with good coping skills.

Partnerships with families benefit all and serve the child better than when professionals and families work separately to provide early care and education. The family knows their child in a different way from the way the professional knows the child. They have information about the past and present that the professional doesn't have. They have visions of a future. They know the child in a greater number of settings than the professional does. The professional knows about children in general, maybe way more than the family does, but not about this particular child in this family. The professional knows how this child behaves in an early childhood environment among peers and with unrelated adults when away from the families. It takes all this information, knowledge, and experience coming together to give the best care and education to each child.

When children see that their teacher or caregiver is working together with their family, they feel more secure. The more they work together the more likely there is to be consistency between what goes on at home and what goes on in the center or at school. The child is likely to feel more comfortable when away from home if the care and education setting is in harmony with the home. The younger the child, the more important the consistency. It's hard for very young children to understand that they should behave differently in one place than they behave in another, though children do grow to have that understanding. The question is, is it good for every child to have to adjust to what may feel like an alien setting at first?

Professionals gain from putting effort into building partnerships by learning more about family differences and traditions. They gain anthropological information as they experience cultural differences. They can do a better job and achieve more satisfaction when they put themselves in partnership with parents.

Taking a partnership approach benefits parents and other family members by giving them a greater understanding of how early childhood education works in general and in this program specifically. By getting involved in the program they gain increased knowledge of their own child in a different setting and can visualize what it is like when they aren't there. They can also carry on at home and expand on what the child is involved in at school or at the center. Parents tend to exhibit self-confidence and feel good about their child expanding his or her horizons and skills as he or she pursues new interests and projects.

There are many strategies for forming partnerships with parents. In fact, every one of the strategies in this book are related to reaching that goal of partnerships. Four more are presented below.

APPROACHES

- If you don't already have support systems, work to create some. To create partnerships with parents you need support from the following:
  - Above—director, principals, board, advisory council
  - In the form of policies and a stated philosophy about the value of partnerships with families and some concrete ways to support it
  - Colleagues you can consult with and talk to
- Find time for communication. Partnerships won't happen if you never have time to talk to parents. This strategy takes more than just a willingness. That's where advocacy comes in (see Strategies 1 and 2). You need support in the form of such things as extra staff, which is a budget issue that you alone can't solve.
- Hone your communication skills. Partnerships depend on clear communication around mutual expectations. Exchange of information is vital to partnerships.
- Figure out a variety of ways to involve parents. The more flexible you are, the more likely you are to get more parents participating.

When children see that their teacher or caregiver is working together with their family, they feel more secure. With a partnership, there is likely to be more consistency between what goes on at home and what goes on in the center.

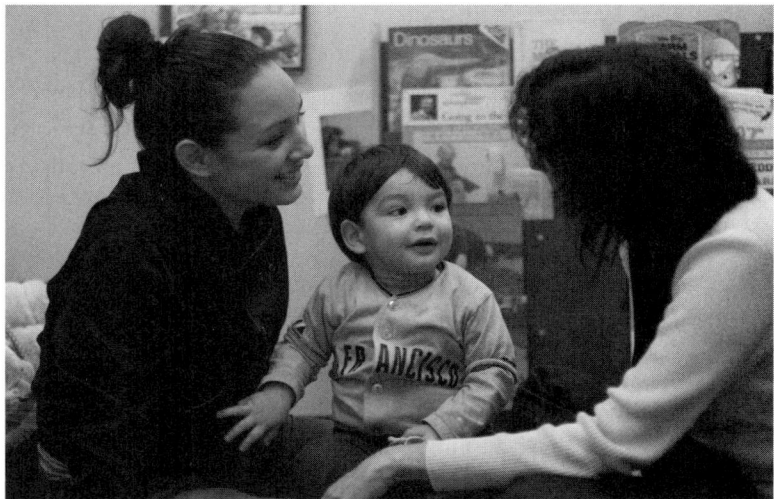

38 SEPARATION: HELPING FAMILIES AND THE CHILDREN

RATIONALE

Helping children and their families with the initial separation in a center or classroom is one issue and is addressed in Strategy 45, Transitions: Helping Parents Help Their Child Enter the Program. But separation issues don't always go away after the first day. Depending on the age of the child and previous experience, parents and children can continue to have painful good-byes every morning for awhile.

Some families come up with a good-bye ritual that helps ease the separation. After they enter the classroom, they do certain things in a certain order before the good-byes are said. In some preschool and infant programs, the program itself has good-bye rituals. Some have a "good-bye" window where the child can stand and wave after the parent walks out.

Sometimes a child arrives for the first time in the early care and education program without any signs of anxiety or fears about separating from her parent. She says good-bye cheerfully and begins to play. That easy separation can go on for some days or even weeks when suddenly separation becomes a painful issue and the child cries and clings. For whatever reason, separation seems to take on new meaning. This is not an unusual situation, although it may startle parents and professionals who haven't experienced it before.

You can help parents and the child with say good-bye by taking the following approaches.

APPROACHES

- If you suffer yourself from children's pain of being separated, you may have unresolved separation issues. Perhaps you are remembering something from your own past that still hurts. We all have had experiences at being apart from the people to whom we are attached. We bring those experiences into the job with us when we work with young children and their families. Self-reflection can do a lot of good when you can bring old pain up to the surface so you can deal with it. Buried, it hurts even more.
- Acknowledge that the pain of separation is real. Don't discount feelings by deciding that this child is just trying to control the situation. Maybe he is, but that's because he wants the pain to stop. When he brightens up soon after the parent leaves, it's tempting to decide that the feelings weren't real. Maybe tuning into your own experience around parting with loved ones will help you understand the child's.
- Sometimes a teacher or caregiver says in a sarcastic tone, "Oh it's the parent who has the problem—the child is fine." That may be the case, but parents deserve empathy too. Criticizing them doesn't help and it drives a wedge in the relationship. Even if they don't hear the ECE professional say the actual words, it's easy to pick up the message in the behaviors.
- Put what you perceive the parent is feeling into words, just as you use words to acknowledge the child's feelings. Be gentle with the parent.
- A parent's ambivalence about leaving can make it harder for the child. Help parents understand how their behaviors can affect their children.
- If parents have a problem separating, what they may need is some guidance on how to do it. That's the caregiver's or teacher's job. Give them some ideas about when is a good time to leave.

Some families come up with a good-bye ritual that helps their children separate from them.

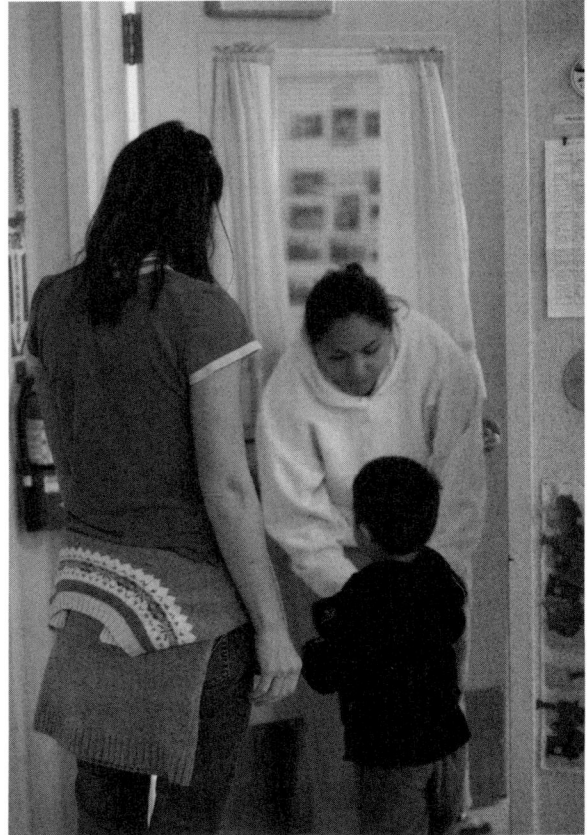

Sometimes the child gets involved in something and then the parent can say good-bye more easily. Even if the child is still crying and the parent has to go, support him or her in the good-byes and encourage the child to walk to the door and wave. There's no one right way to help the parent out the door. Try different things until you find something that works.

A story: One toddler suffered a great deal every time his mother left him at the center. He came on Tuesdays and Thursdays, and both he and his mother began to dread the good-byes. The mother and the teacher talked this over every chance they got, trying to figure out how to help him suffer less. One suggestion the teacher came up with was to enroll him for more than two days a week, but for a shorter day. After the second week, they noticed an improvement, but he was still unhappy about saying good-bye. "I think he continues to be afraid that I'm not coming back," said the mother. One day the mother accidentally left her purse at the center. The teacher put it in the child's cubby. That day he was much happier and more secure. From then on, the mother left her purse (minus wallet and keys). The sight of it in his cubby seemed to reassure the boy that his mother would return—if not for him, at least for her purse!

39

SPECIAL SITUATIONS: DIVORCE IN THE FAMILY

RATIONALE

Special attention is needed for children and families who are going through a divorce, which is a major transition for all the family members. A break-up often involves financial stress as well as a move from the original residence. A lower standard of living for the children may also be a result. This period may bring feelings of loss as one parent is no longer as much a part of the children's life. Sometimes the siblings are split up. The original family no long exists in the same way. There may be a long unsettled period in which life is not predictable and a sense of security is disrupted. The rocky period usually starts before the actual divorce occurs as parents go through a period (long or short) of conflict.

APPROACHES

- Examine your own attitudes and feelings about divorce. Become aware of any stereotypes you may have of families who are undergoing this transition or the consequences for children. It is different for each family and each person in the family. The process of the divorce may make for difficult times and correspondingly difficult behavior, but don't decide that you already know the long time effects on the children. Many of the ideas about negative outcomes do not hold true. Children are not necessarily worse off because their parents divorce, nor are they worse off living in single-parent families than in two-parent families. There are many myths and misconceptions about children of divorced parents.
- Though you can't do anything about the tensions being felt at home, you can help parents deal with their children's feelings and resulting behaviors, which may include fears, sleep disturbance, fussing, and whining. Sometimes children regress—go back to an earlier time in their life and pick up old behaviors that they had shed long ago, such as bedwetting or thumb sucking. The ordinarily easy-to-get-along-with child may become demanding, defiant, or disobedient. The usually secure child may become dependent and show separation anxiety. In playtimes you may notice less positive interaction, more aggression, and perhaps less involvement as the usually active child becomes more of an observer. Older children may look sad, have difficulty focusing, and show fear, anxiety, or anger.

Even a divorce can have some light spots. This child may be indicating that rain can result in rainbows.

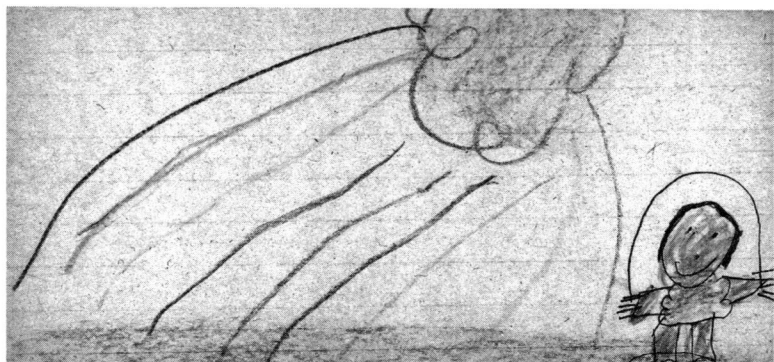

- Sometimes children can come to the conclusion that the divorce was their fault. It's important that they understand that that is not true and they are not to be blamed.
- Of course, parents have their own feelings and although you are not a therapist, you can still offer them support. You can't meet their needs, but you can listen to them if they feel like talking. On the other hand, they may not feel like talking. They may be so upset that they turn away and become less interactive with the teacher or caregiver. Understanding and empathy are the best response to changes in parental attitudes and behavior during this difficult period.
- There are community resources for families in stress. Know what they are and make information available for the parents. You can't be all things to all people, but you can point family members toward the help they might need for counseling. Parents without Partners can be a support for them too. Have contact information available.
- Make available books about divorce—for both children and adults.
- Be very clear about who is authorized to pick up the children and who is not.
- Know that this period will pass. Be kind, gentle, and understanding.

40

SPECIAL SITUATIONS: FAMILIES REFERRED FOR ABUSING OR NEGLECTING THEIR CHILDREN

RATIONALE

Abuse and neglect are heartbreaking conditions for anyone to face, yet every day children who are victims of such treatment come into early care and education programs along with their families. Legal definitions of abuse and neglect differ by state, but in general, abuse is characterized by mistreatment that results in physical harm or is likely to harm the child. Physical abuse includes spanking *only* if the child is bruised or injured in some other way. Sexual abuse includes any form of sexual conduct in which children are used to provide sexual gratification for the perpetrator. Also included as sexual abuse are any forms of sexual exploitation including child pornography. Emotional abuse is harder to see, but it relates to rejection, isolation, and corruption of a child. Terrorizing is a form of emotional abuse. Even ignoring a child under certain circumstances can be considered emotional abuse. Emotional abuse includes such widely ranging examples as allowing a child to engage in criminal activity, inattention to a child's need for psychological help, verbal abuse, and exposing a child to domestic violence. Neglect falls into a different category of abuse and is characterized by refusal to meet basic needs including affection and attention or withholding health care.

It may seem as if abuse and neglect happen just among low-income families, but that's not true. Abuse and neglect happen at all levels of society, although maltreatment occurs more often to children who have disabilities. There are some risk factors that should be considered. Certainly poverty can cause stress, and stress can cause abuse. Isolation of the family from others can be another risk factor. The coping skills of the family and lack of anger management can contribute to the possibility of abuse. Health issues in the family can result in the neglect of a child. Characteristics of the actual child can be a factor in abuse and neglect. When several of these factors work together, the family is more vulnerable. Knowing the families you work with may help you direct some to support services and prevent abuse before it happens.

Anyone who works with young children is a mandated reporter and by law must report any suspected abuse or neglect. You don't have to prove it—just suspect it. If you suspect abuse, be sure you have your facts straight and have some kind of grounds for your suspicions. Don't do anything with the family yourself. In your program there may be a reporting procedure—an authority to go to as the second step—the director, the principal, the school social worker. Finally, call your local child protection agency to report.

If families have been referred to your program after having been identified by authorities as having maltreated their children, it is your job to work with them. You may have feelings about their children and what they have been through, but nevertheless you need to approach the families with the same openness, acceptance, and respect with which you approach any other family. It may be a challenge to do that, but that's what is needed. In the long run, everybody benefits.

APPROACHES

- Becoming aware of your own feelings and attitudes is important. You may feel angry with a parent for an injury she caused to her child, but your job is to get to know her and work to understand, respect, and support her.

- Build a trusting relationship with all parents, including those who have been referred for abuse or neglect. It may be especially difficult because you are a mandated reporter and parents know that. They may not see you "on their side." It is important that you work as hard to relate to them as you do to any other parents or family members. One way to show that you are trustworthy is to keep confidentiality. Do not talk about a family to others.
- Don't assume that children who have been abused and neglected no longer feel close to their parent(s). Attachment usually holds up even in extremely abusive circumstances. Be very careful that you do not say anything negative to children about their parents. Show them that you support both them and their parents.
- Help prevent abuse by doing the following:
  - Providing support when needed or referring to outside sources of support. If parents have been referred to your program because of their problems with abuse or neglect, it is likely that they already are connected with a support group. For other families under stress, keep up to date on community resource information. Know the numbers for parental hotlines, family support centers, crisis centers, parent support groups, Parents Anonymous, and counseling and parent education programs. Preventing abuse and neglect is a much better approach than addressing it after it occurs.
  - Offering ideas for increasing parenting skills, such as guidance approaches using problem-solving strategies and approaches rather than physical punishment.
  - Modeling nonviolent and nonaggressive conflict-resolution approaches in the classroom with the children.
  - Working with children who lack social skills to improve them. Some child behaviors put them at risk for being abused in families that have other risk factors as well.

This excerpt from a preschool parent handbook is a fairly standard statement about the legal mandate that early care and education professionals have to report suspected child abuse. In some programs, families enrolling their children are required to sign a statement that they understand that suspected child abuse will be reported to the authorities.

15

Menus

Monthly menus are posted in the kitchen area in both centers and on the bulletin boards near the entry doors. Menus are available to parents upon request.

Food Allergies

Be sure to notify us of any food allergies. Food allergies are listed on the front of the child's nametag and on lists posted in the children's eating areas and on the refrigerators.

Minor modifications can be made to many of our menus to meet the needs of children with allergies (e.g. burritos with no cheese or white flour tortillas instead of whole wheat). Parents with children with extreme food allergies should ask for menus to determine any day when their child is unable to eat what is being served. On that day, the parent needs to bring a main course item for the child. It should be marked and given to a staff member.

Other Allergies

Pets and regular outside play are parts of our daily curriculum. If your child has an extreme allergy, please let us know.

Child Abuse

All employees of the DVC Developmental Children's Center are mandated to report suspected instances of child abuse, mental suffering or endangerment of the emotional well being of children that they become aware of in their professional capacity, or within the scope of their employment.

We want to work with all of the adults whether they are parents, staff or students associated with our Center to keep children safe and healthy. Additional helpful information is available from the Family Stress Center in Concord (925/827-0212) or the Contra Costa County Child Abuse Prevention Council (925/946-9961).

41
SPECIAL SITUATIONS: GRANDPARENTS AS PARENTS

RATIONALE

Steven Thaxton (2003) has worked with grandparents who are parenting their children's children, as have many other early childhood educators. This group has some special issues that other families don't have. They also have different needs and different strengths.

Most of them have a sad story to tell. The reasons they have custody of their grandchildren varies, but there's a sad history somewhere. Parents die, go to jail, disappear, are physically disabled, or are mentally disabled. The stories go on and on. Most grandparents thought once they raised their children that parenting was over—at least the intense kind of parenting necessary for younger children. To learn otherwise is a shock to some.

Thaxton was surprised to find out through interviewing grandparents that they had what he called an "undying" love for their grandchildren. "They talk about how wonderful the children are, and how much they want for their lives to be better; they know the children's lives will be better since they are living with their grandparents. They can provide consistency and loving relationships that the children are missing from their parents."

But there is also a lot of sadness and worry. They may still be mourning the loss of their own children. They worry about medical issues and legal problems. They are concerned about what will happen to the children if something happens to them. They worry that they don't fit in at school because they are so much older than the other family members who attend meetings and get involved.

Thaxton offers some strategies that can help grandparents feel a part of the early care and education program their grandchildren attend.

APPROACHES

- Don't be judgmental. Grandparents may not understand how the early care and education system works, so plan time to spend with them to explain programs, policies, regulations, and the availability of services. This is what you'd expect to do with any parent who came into the program for the first time. The fact that the parent is a grandparent shouldn't make any difference.
- Grandparents may have lots of questions. They may have been involved with systems that weren't friendly. They may ask why about a lot of things. Answer their questions.
- Like with any parent, you should aim to become a partner with the grandparents.
- Take time to listen to their stories. They have lived long and been through a lot. They'll be glad to know that they have found someone who is understanding and empathetic.
- Encourage grandparents to participate. Find out what their strengths are and let them participate in their own way at their own level.
- Ask what they need and then help them get it. Some may require respite care—either provide it or help them find it.
- Treat them with the same respect and understanding that you treat other parents.

42

SPECIAL SITUATIONS: PARENTS WHO APPEAR HOSTILE

RATIONALE

Let's look at a parent who is often angry, aggressive, and seems to harbor deep hostility. This is a parent who presents real challenges to many early childhood professionals. Those of us who work with young children may have a tendency to be nice and want others to be nice also. That's not true of all of us, but it is an impression one gets when in the field for very long. Teachers, caregivers, and staff who like "nice" may give up on working with what they consider to be a hostile parent. Interestingly enough, most teachers don't give upon children as readily as they do parents. In fact, some teachers energize themselves to take on a challenging child while they want to turn their back on an angry parent. Some even want to run away and hide! Worse, some give up on all parents because of a few difficult experiences. (See Strategy 7, Attitudes of Professionals.)

APPROACHES

- Avoid labeling parents or anybody else. The labels can get in the way of your ability to work with them.
- Separate your feelings from the parents' like you do with children. Notice when defensive or aggressive feelings arise in you. Getting angry in the face of anger is not usually an effective responsive if this is a person with whom you are trying to establish a relationship. An experienced professional learns to step aside from a child's anger and not take it personally. Most can acknowledge the feelings without getting caught up in them. Just as we do that for children, we can learn to do that for adults.
- Try to accept the feelings and understand them if you can. Don't overanalyze; you aren't a therapist, but do realize that, for example, a parent's strong feelings may relate to genuine concern for her child. A parent may lack skills for communicating concerns. Instead of being assertive about what's bothering her, she may use aggression instead. Sometimes behavior comes out the opposite of what the feeling is. People with low self-esteem act conceited and people who feel powerless can become pushy. People who are afraid may exhibit anger instead.
- Recognize that strong feelings are not usually about whatever triggers them but have deeper roots. Fear and grief may well show up as anger toward someone who has nothing to do with what makes the angry person afraid or puts him in mourning.
- Your job is to remain calm and work to open up communication by becoming aware of what blocks communication, such as:
  - Defensive responses
  - Arguing
  - Criticizing
  - Distracting
- Practice what has long been called *active listening,* a time-honored strategy used by early childhood educators. Thomas Gordon (2000) named this strategy in his book *Parent Effectiveness Training.* Originally designed to use with children, active listening also works well with adults. It is a way of acknowledging feelings so the other person realizes that you are accepting them

rather than criticizing them or trying to make them go away. Put into nonjudgmental words what you perceive. The trick is to hit the nail on the head. If you say, "You seem irritated," and the parent is furious, you missed the mark. At least if he or she corrects you, you've got a start on communication.

- Realize that the time and effort you put into working with an angry parent may result in your meeting up with the nice person underneath the angry cover.

43

STRENGTHS: FOCUS ON

RATIONALE

When a family you are trying to build a relationship with is struggling with many challenges, you try to empathize with them. You seek to understand what it is like to walk in their shoes. Perhaps, at the same time, you think about the ways you can help them and also consider the resources the community has to offer them. All these approaches are valid, but they also lead you to focus on the family's problems instead of its strengths. Turnbull and Turnbull (2001) said, "Highlighting and appreciating families' strengths is one of the key aspects of supporting families to enhance their own self-efficacy" (p. 67).

A key to working with all families is to be sensitive, understanding, empathetic, *and* remember their strengths. You're not a therapist, but you can be an ally. Just by listening and talking, you can show your support. By having faith in people to use their abilities to succeed in life in spite of obstacles, you can help them heal. Think about people in your own life who have believed in your strengths and recognized your potential.

It may be hard to shift focus from problems to strengths, but think about the following approaches that you can take to make such a shift.

"Highlighting and appreciating families' strengths is one of the key aspects of supporting families to enhance their own self-efficacy" (Turnbull & Turnbull, 2001).

APPROACHES

- Look at how you are defining the family. Can you see how they are unique and special instead of downtrodden and miserable? Are you aware of the skills, strengths, and special talents each member has? Think about their resources.
- If you don't know enough about the family to see its strengths, do you have ways to find out? Having conversations with the members is one way. You may not have much time to talk to families, but if you are dedicated to partnerships with parents, you know that conversations are essential if you are to get to know and appreciate each family.
- Storytelling is another way to learn about family strengths. When we hear each other's stories, it makes us remember our own. Stories can be healing. Just remember as you listen to stories, you can think in terms of possibilities instead of dwelling on problems.
- The challenges individuals and families face do not necessarily weaken them, but sometimes they give them the strength and courage to grow, develop, and move forward. Don't assume that challenges always result in damage.
- Help the family keep their focus on their dreams and aspirations instead of what is happening right now. Help them concentrate on life without the challenges they face at the moment. If they can visualize that life, they can aim for it.
- You may have expertise, but the real experts in this family are the members themselves. Help them tune in to the expertise they have.

Perhaps the child who drew this picture comes from a family that has a love of music as one of its strengths.

- Help them empower themselves by making them aware of the choices they have. (See Strategy 24, Empowerment.)
- You may have resources to offer them, but help them tune in on their own resources and focus on their strengths, skills, and potentials.
- Focus on protective factors rather than on risk factors. For example, a family who has a broad base of support for the parents and is a member of a community has an important protective factor to stand up against the risk factor of ill health or a financial crisis.

What are some strengths that families show even when they have big problems? Here are some samples of strengths families can have—either as a group or as individuals within the family:

1. Strong attachment that shows up as love for their children and is reciprocated.
2. An extended family network that they can rely on.
3. The ability to speak two languages plus one dialect.
4. Good social skills.
5. Persistence and stubbornness. They don't give up.
6. Physical strength, body awareness, good health habits.
7. A strong sense of humor.
8. A love of making music and listening to it.
9. A cheerful outlook.
10. A variety of interests.
11. "Street smarts." They know how to get along and keep safe.
12. Mutual support.
13. A knowledge of how to "work the system."

44 TALKING WITH FAMILIES WHEN CONCERNS ARISE

RATIONALE

Teachers and caregivers are often the first to notice that a child moves, behaves, interacts, learns, or communicates differently from other children. When you observe that you are not able to meet the child's needs, support his or her development, or foster his or her sense of belonging in the program, you may decide that the child needs more expertise than you have. That's an indication that this is the time to have a meeting with the parents.

If you have a relationship with the parents and have been talking to them all along, the meeting about your concerns may not come as a surprise. It's quite possible that the parents, too, have been concerned and are glad to share their observations when they hear yours. Come in to the meeting with notes on what you have observed and what kinds of interventions you may have tried. Here are some suggestions for conducting the meeting.

APPROACHES

- Before putting together a meeting with the family in which you plan to discuss the possibility of getting outside help, do a series of observations. Note specifies. Objectively and in detail describe behaviors that you have seen—the ones that give you cause for concern. Note when and where those behaviors occurred and under what circumstances. In conjunction with your observations, see if changing the environment or your approach affects the behavior. This is important information to share with the parents. Remember it is only appropriate for you to discuss what you have observed about specific behaviors. Avoid the urge to label or diagnose.
- In the meeting itself, try to make the parents feel comfortable and at ease as much as possible. Choose a seating arrangement that brings you together instead of separating you. Sitting behind a desk, for example, can make a psychological as well as a physical barrier between you and the parents. A warmer, friendlier arrangement may work better. Provide for privacy. Set aside enough time so that the meeting isn't rushed and you can talk things through. If this is the first such meeting the parents have had, they need to feel that you care and that they can trust you.
- Start by asking the family how they see their child and share any positive qualities you have observed. At the outset, let the family know that you are sharing your concerns to support their child's development and to get some ideas for how to best meet their child's needs. If the family differs in their view of the child, be open to their perspective, ask questions, gather information, and invite them to be your partner in meeting the needs of their child.
- Before you share your concerns with them, ask if they have any that they haven't already indicated. When it is time to share your concerns, be sure you communicate what you want to say clearly, without judgment and with concrete examples. For example, rather than saying that a child is "behaving badly and bothering other children," give specifics—let the parents know that you have observed and documented that their child has a harder time sitting still than other children, doesn't cope well with transitions, and has had five incidents of hitting other children during the last week. DO NOT suggest that a child has a specific diagnosis (such as attention deficit disorder).

- If the parents don't understand your concerns or disagree with you, they may be upset if you suggest that a referral for further assessment is necessary. It's possible that your observations will shock or anger them. In this case, sensitively supporting the parents' feelings is called for. Just as when infants and toddlers are distressed, caregivers accept the feelings and empathize with the child, so parents need the same approach from caregivers. You're not a therapist, but some of the listening skills of a therapist can serve you well. Understanding that anger or blame are common responses for people in pain helps you accept the feelings without getting defensive. The point is to focus on the feelings of the parents and listen to what they have to say without minimizing their upset or trying to talk them out of it.

- Keep clear that further assessment is a positive move and that both you and the parents have the child's best interests at heart even if you don't see eye-to-eye at the moment.

- Sometimes the family may not choose to access resources when you first share your concerns, or they may be open to information yet not take action immediately. Rather than label them as being "in denial" or something else, remember that everyone moves at a different pace and accepts information differently. The family's emotional response will affect what they are able to hear and understand. Processing and integrating this information will take varying amounts of time.

- Allow families time to accept that their child may be different than other children. That possibility is very hard for some families to hear. Unless there is a reason for urgency, let the family to proceed on their own time line.

- Be prepared to support them in understanding what you have shared, repeating the information whenever necessary. Let them know that there is resource information available whenever they want it. If you find that your own judgment or emotions about this interfere with your ability to respect the family as the decision-maker, seek support for yourself and don't be afraid to suggest that the family discuss this with someone else as well.

- Support the family in getting help. Let them know that you are there for them and for their child. If it comes to contacting an early intervention program, local school district, or pediatrician/healthcare provider, let the family take the lead.

- Since many families will want to take action, be prepared to talk with them about resources for obtaining further assessment and/or possible services. This is the point at which you are "making a referral." It is generally appropriate to refer the family to their pediatrician at the same time you refer them to the local early intervention/special education resources. You should have information about services within your program, local early intervention services, special education services, and other resources.

- You cannot guarantee eligibility or services from another agency to a family. You can describe what might happen after the referral and what the possible outcomes might be based on what you've learned. You can also let the family know that you can be a source of information to the referral source. Parents must give permission for you to talk about their child with referral sources, so you will want to carefully respect the family's confidentiality and be sure that you have clear consent.

- When accessing resources, the family may face some barriers including issues of insurance, language, cultural practices, and transportation. It's okay for you to set the process in motion for them, but rather than feeling responsible for overcoming all the barriers, focus on supporting the family and have faith that by finding their own ways to meet their child's needs you serve the family and their child best (Brault, in press).

45 TRANSITIONS: HELPING PARENTS HELP THEIR CHILD ENTER THE PROGRAM

RATIONALE

Preparations for the first day can start ahead of time when parents know that they will be leaving children for short periods with people outside the family. The parents can help the children get used to separation in small doses. Often the children who have the most trouble separating upon entering an early childhood program are those who are away from family for the first time, although that is not always true. Ideally, the child also has some familiarity with the teacher or caregiver before the first day. (See Strategy 29, First Meeting with Families.) Those programs that are fully dedicated to partnering with parents sometimes figure out how to make home visits to the family before they start the program. (See Strategy 30, Home Visits.) This not only serves to meet the family on its home territory, but also the child who is being enrolled. Another option is to invite the child and family to visit the program so the child can meet the teacher or caregiver and become familiar with the setting. Either one of those approaches ensures that the child doesn't enter the first day to a strange place with a strange adult.

Some programs invite the parents to help their child enter the program for the first time by encouraging them to stay until the child is comfortable. This kind of invitation sets a warm tone and gives messages to both the child and family member that this is their place and they are welcome. This first experience can encourage parents to get involved in the program. Although some ECE professionals would prefer the parents to drop off their children and leave right away, there are some advantages in letting parents who can and want to stay to do so.

A common situation is for a parent to want to sneak out without saying good-bye because she knows her child will cling and cry. It is best to discuss the possibility of this situation ahead of time rather than address it when it happens. The ECE professional can show empathy for a parent who has feelings about her child's separation behaviors. At the same time she can help the parent understand that it is harder on the child when they come to distrust the parent than it is to express their feelings about separation openly.

Of course, when a child has been in early care and education programs from a young age, he may be quite used to separation, although the first day of kindergarten or first grade may be a bigger one than he is used to. It may be a new setting with new regulations. The group's size may be larger, and having parents in the classroom on the first day isn't as feasible as in programs for younger children.

APPROACHES

- Reassure parents that the child is in good hands.
- Demonstrate acceptance of feelings—both the child's and the parent's. It helps if they can both see that their upset doesn't upset you too.
- Help parents see that separation anxiety is quite common and nothing to worry about. Indeed, it shows attachment and that's a good thing. Some parents may take protesting behavior as bad manners. Assure them that you don't see it that way.
- Suggest to the parent to allow the child to decide when the parent can leave. Although this doesn't always work, when it does, it gives the child a sense of self-confidence.
- Pair a new child with another child. Pair the parent with another more experienced parent.
- Allow "transition objects," something special from home that the child finds comfort in when the separation issues get her down.

Good-byes the first day can be hard. Accept the child's feelings and try pairing him up with another child. Notice the teacher is down at eye level with the children when she talks to them.

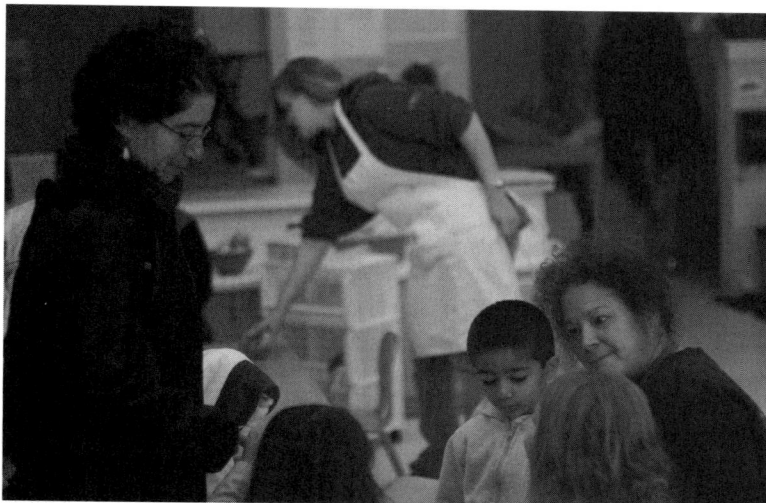

Under the section "Daily Guidelines" in this parent handbook, there are some ideas and also some specific instructions under a subsection called "Bringing Your Child."

DAILY GUIDELINES

→ **Bringing Your Child**

It is important to help your child make the transition from home to school. If a staff member has not greeted your child, take your child to one of the teachers. State licensing requires that teachers greet children and their parents and assess the health of the child before the parent leaves.

A few things to remember:

1. You may bring your child ten minutes before the block begins. This gives some time for greeting the teacher, looking around the school with your child, and walking to your class.

2. Sign your child in on the daily sign-in sheet when you arrive. You must use a complete signature.

3. Pin your child's nametag on and assist in hanging up his or her coat.

4. Let teachers know any information that will help them as they work with your child (lack of sleep, change in daily schedule, new medicine, et cetera).

Leaving with Your Child

1. Sign your child out when you pick him/her up. Only persons listed on the Emergency Card may pick up a child. The parent of record must inform the staff verbally and give written permission if someone else is picking-up the child. The person picking-up must check-in with the Children's Center Office and present photo identification before the child can be released.

2. Leave your child's nametag in the place designated by your child's teacher.

3. Check your child's cubby for treasures waiting to go home.

4. Take home wet clothes.

5. If your child has worn DVC extra clothing home, please clean and return it the next day you attend school.

6. CHECK YOUR PARENT MAILBOX. PLEASE READ AND RESPOND TO ANY MEMOS OR NOTICES.

A story about starting kindergarten: Nicky was born prematurely, got a rocky start in life, and was medically fragile for the first two years of his life. He had experience in two different early care and education settings before starting kindergarten. Each time he began a new program, his parent stayed until he was comfortable staying by himself. Kindergarten was a big step after preschool, and Nicky started worrying. Before school started, he attended a parent meeting with his mother. When the teacher announced that the children would stay in the classroom while the parents took a tour of the school grounds, Nicky grabbed his mother's hand and wouldn't let go. He was the only child that day who got the school grounds tour with the parents. The mother talked to the teacher when the meeting was over to tell her that she always stayed with Nicky in school until he felt comfortable when entering a new program. The teacher was very clear when she said in a firm voice, "No parents in the classroom the first day." Both Nicky and his mother were worried about the first day. They had a talk. His mother explained that this new school had new rules and even though neither of them liked the one about no parents in the classroom, that's just the way it was. "So what are you going to do?" she asked him. He thought about it for awhile and then said, "I'll go under the table." Once he had a strategy, he felt a lot braver. The first day came and he let go of his mother's hand and walked straight into the classroom. After the session she picked him up and was glad to see a big smile on his face. "How did it go?" she asked. "Well," he said. "I did just what I said. I went under the table. Then a girl said, 'teacher there's a boy under the table.' So I came out." That's all he ever said about it, but apparently the strategy worked! The second day he came up with a new strategy. He wore his Superman tee shirt.

46 TRANSITIONS: MANAGING THE END OF THE DAY

RATIONALE

Reconnecting children with their families at the end of the session or day has its own issues. Everybody is likely to be tired and short on patience. Children may be disappointed that the parent hasn't come sooner. The last child there may be anxious that he has been forgotten. Lots of things are going on at the end of the day. The ideal is when the parent arrives, the child jumps up delighted and runs to gather his things. That sometimes happens, but not always. Children react to their parents' return in many different ways. One way is to just keep on playing and ignore the fact that the parent is there and it is time to go home.

One phenomenon that can cause parents pain is fairly common. It's this: A child who protested at his parent leaving him in the morning resists going home when the parent arrives for him in the afternoon. That may seem strange. There are several possible explanations. One might be that the child has difficulty with transitions and both arrival and departure times represent transitions. The parent may already know this about his child and if he observed during the day he would see the same thing happening at school as happens at home. The child resists getting into the bathtub and then resists getting

The ideal is when the parent arrives and the child, even though tired, comes right into waiting arms. That sometimes happens, but not always. The end of the day can be a time of stress for everybody—families, children, and teachers.

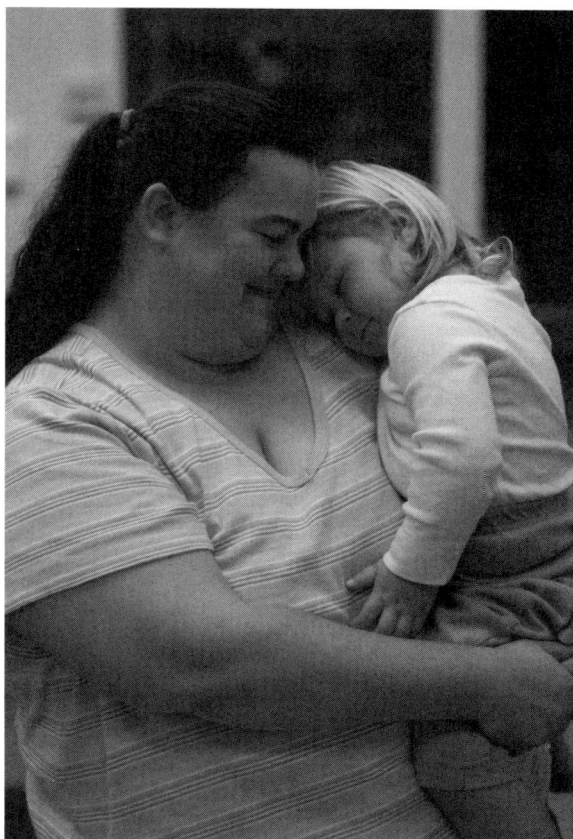

out when the bath is over. When it's time to go outdoors at school, he wants to remain inside, but once he gets outside he doesn't want to come back in again. This is a temperament issue.

There could be a very different explanation about why the child doesn't want to go home. When he is left in the morning, he may feel angry and resentful. Even though he enjoys being in the program, he feels abandoned when the parent leaves. Those angry feelings may brew throughout the day and bubble over when the child sees the parent again in the afternoon. Maybe by resisting going home, the child is punishing the parent.

Another simple explanation is that the child is in the middle of something and doesn't want to leave it.

When a child makes a fuss about going home when it is time to leave, his behavior can trigger feelings in parents. Disappointment and hurt can come when the parent arrives anticipating the child would be happy to see her. He doesn't love me any more may be the parent's thought. He doesn't need me! He loves his teacher more than me. These thoughts can create great insecurity in a parent. Or maybe the parent feels embarrassed about the child's behavior—thinking the teacher will consider the child rude and unmannerly and the parent inadequate because she hasn't done a good job of raising the child.

Maybe the child is just overtired after a busy, stimulating, and interesting day. Worn-out children can end up crying over any little thing. They just fall apart. Without knowing what's really going on with the child, parents can jump to conclusions about why the child is acting out.

Teachers, caregivers, and family child care providers can also jump to conclusions about why the child doesn't seem to want to go home, especially the first time they run into this situation. They might assume the child prefers the teacher to the parent. (See Strategy 17, Competition: Parents and

The same parent handbook also has some specific instructions under a subsection called "Leaving with Your Child."

7

A few things to remember:

1. You may bring your child ten minutes before the block begins. This gives some time for greeting the teacher, looking around the school with your child, and walking to your class.

2. Sign your child in on the daily sign-in sheet when you arrive. You must use a complete signature.

3. Pin your child's nametag on and assist in hanging up his or her coat.

4. Let teachers know any information that will help them as they work with your child (lack of sleep, change in daily schedule, new medicine, et cetera).

→ **Leaving with Your Child**

1. Sign your child out when you pick him/her up. Only persons listed on the Emergency Card may pick up a child. The parent of record must inform the staff verbally and give written permission if someone else is picking-up the child. The person picking-up must check-in with the Children's Center Office and present photo identification before the child can be released.

2. Leave your child's nametag in the place designated by your child's teacher.

3. Check your child's cubby for treasures waiting to go home.

4. Take home wet clothes.

5. If your child has worn DVC extra clothing home, please clean and return it the next day you attend school.

6. CHECK YOUR PARENT MAILBOX. PLEASE READ AND RESPOND TO ANY MEMOS OR NOTICES.

Clothing

Children play best when dressed for the occasion. We ask you to follow these guidelines:

1. Dress children in clothing that can be removed easily and, it possible, independently and that is suitable for the weather conditions. Play clothes should

Professionals.) Or maybe they jump to the conclusion that there's something very wrong at home. They may decide that the child is afraid of the parent and that must mean there is abuse going on. Making the wrong assumption can cause some serious difficulties with building a trusting relationship if the teacher decides to act on them.

Experienced teachers aren't surprised at this kind of behavior at the end of the day. They have seen it often enough to understand that it can stem from many sources. They can help the parent understand it too.

Here are some ways you can have the children more ready to meet their parents in better shape.

APPROACHES

- Make an end-of-the-day routine or ritual, if possible, so the children know what to expect.
- Let things wind down. Have activities available, but don't bring out your best wild activities right before going home time.
- Be aware of pacing throughout the session or day. Have periods of quiet and rest alternating with active periods. Also have spaces in the environment where children who need rest and down time can go to find it. Be aware of which children are likely to get overstimulated and end up exhausted and try to regulate their activity so they are still fresh by the end.
- If children don't all leave at the same time, figure out what to do with the last child—the one who stays longer than the others. This child may become unhappy and feel like she is being abandoned if alone for very long. Put some thought into making this a good time for her, whether it's some special activity, time she gets you to herself, or whatever.
- Help parents understand the many reasons why a child might not run into their open arms when they arrive to take them home. For example:
  - The child who barely looks up may be one who is so secure in his attachment and so clear that his parents always come for him that he just finishes up what he is doing. Older children are quite likely to react this way at the end of the day when it's time to go home. They don't worry about separation because they've been having reunions for a long time and they are used to them.
  - The child who is engrossed in something may protest when the parents urge him to leave because he wants to continue what he is doing.
  - Some children immediately begin to break the rules when the parent arrives. It may be that they are testing who is in charge. (See Strategy 9, Authority.)
  - The child who falls apart may do so because he's been on his best behavior all day and now that the people he feels most comfortable with are here, he just lets go.

47 TRANSITIONS: MOVING ON

RATIONALE

One of the hardest parts of parenting is keeping up with children moving from one stage to another. The most dramatic moves come in the first two years. A parent gets used to having a baby and knows about how to take care of it. Then the baby gets up on all fours and starts moving around and the parent is faced with a whole new set of behaviors and a need to childproof the home. The changes come rapidly. Some parents are surprised when their infant, who consumed amazing quantities of food, becomes a toddler who eats practically nothing. If they don't adjust to the fact that since the growth rate slowed down, the child needs far less food, they may continue to try to get him to eat more. That can result in an eating problem or at least a power struggle. Some timely parenting tips from the staff at the center can serve as prevention for later problems.

Here's where effective parent education can come in. Parents can learn about the new behaviors they need to match those of the new stage. One place to learn them is from their ECE program. If they observe, they can probably see children who are already in the next stage beyond their child. Also they can watch how the staff responds to behaviors that may be new to the parents. Talking to other parents in the program can help too. This kind of parent education is a big benefit of ECE programs for parents.

The next challenge for parents is learning to guide behavior and to set limits (which they will probably call "discipline" until they learn different terminology from their ECE program). An immobile infant has natural limits. Guidance isn't an issue, but once he can get around and develops a mind of his own, guidance becomes essential. How does a parent make the transition between just accepting what the infant does to working with a defiant toddler? Some need help. That's where the ECE program and the professionals in it can be a big help to parents. Parent education becomes something sought after at this stage by many parents. Articles to read, discussion groups, even lectures and videos are gratefully received by families who are facing a new stage with which they aren't familiar.

APPROACHES

- Take your position as a parent educator seriously. Just as you respond to the care and education of children as individuals, so should you respond to parents as individuals. Some parents are new at parenting and they may be real beginners without ever having been around children before. They are most likely eager to know more, especially if they perceive you as a resource and not a threat—as someone who can give them ideas, but not criticize them. Other parents may be much more experienced at parenting. They can also be resources to parents who need skills, information, and support.
- There are many ways to facilitate learning. Just as ECE professionals pay attention to the different learning styles of children, so they can pay attention to those of parents and other family members. What works best? It could be articles tucked into the parent's mailbox in response to questions asked; discussions around a topic that a parent or group of parents show interest in; a lending library with a variety of materials on lots of subjects related to parenting; a list of suggested readings; observations followed by discussion; videos; and pairing experienced parents with inexperienced ones are just a few ideas of how to match teaching approaches and resources to individual learning styles.

Moving from stage to stage is one aspect of moving on. Moving from one classroom to another or from one program to another is another aspect of moving on. In some programs the moving from one stage to another means a move in the program as well. One infant-toddler center that had a goal of developmentally appropriate environments set up a system where every time a child reached a new stage of development he or she moved to a new classroom with a new teacher. That meant four different moves in the first year for children who arrived in the program early in life. When you consider the issue of relationships—baby and caregiver as well as parents and caregiver—the constant transitioning can be very unsettling. So what are some strategies for helping parents help their children to move on whether changing programs, changing teachers, or changing classrooms? Here are some suggestions.

APPROACHES

- Transitions should be slow and not occur too often. Some children suffer greatly even with a small transition like from one activity to another. They resist change—even little changes. They don't like new things. Other children are less reluctant, but transitions create some stress in almost all children.
- Remember that with every transition children make, the family is also affected. Moving on is felt by everybody.
- One strategy for making transitions in early care and education settings, especially for infants and toddlers who are ready to move on, is to have the adult move with the children. It is important for both the child and the family to develop a trusting relationship with a particular caregiver and once established, it should continue. Called continuity of care by WestEd's Program for Infant-Toddler Caregivers (PITC), this system recognizes the importance of attachment and the stability of long-term connections.
- If the caregiver or teacher can't move with the children, at least have the children stay together as a group. They can support each other through the transition. That's different from the practice where individuals move up to another group when they reach a certain birthday. It's also different from programs where the aim is for children to constantly meet new children by mixing groups up every time they move to a new level, class, or grade.
- Consider the advantage of a family child care home as an early care and education setting when it comes to lowering the number of transitions. Some family child care providers have several children from the same family and may stay connected with the family for years. Children come as newborn babies into a family child care home and may be there until they outgrow early care and education! In some cases, the child grows up, has children of his own, and sends them to the same provider he went to in his early years. Talk about long-term relationships and continuity of care!

A story: One infant-toddler program decided to institute a continuity of care system where babies stayed with the same caregivers until they were old enough to move to preschool, which was housed in the same building. The caregivers stayed with the group, even though the environment changed as the babies outgrew the room they started out in. The first time around, nobody knew exactly how this would work, and some were doubtful that it would. There was some resistance on the part of the caregivers because they were used to a certain age group and didn't think they would like working with older or younger children. But that turned out not to be a problem once they got connected to the babies. They really enjoyed "moving up with them" and seeing more of the developmental sequence unfold. By the time the first group was almost old enough to transition to preschool and leave the infant-toddler staff behind, there was some concern about the separation process. After being with the same caregiver for so long, wouldn't they suffer when they said good-bye? The surprise was that the children did great. They were excited about becoming preschoolers and the transition was slow enough that they got used to the preschool room and teachers before the final move came. The new world and people in it were so interesting and exciting to them that the separation was a gentle one. Even the caregivers found letting go easy because they felt the children were ready to move on and they knew they would continue to see them. They just wouldn't be their caregivers any more. The other surprise was that the group who suffered separation anxieties were the parents! They worried a good deal about the new teacher and the new program. They just didn't want to let go of the people they had grown to know and trust!

48 TREATING ALL FAMILIES WITH RESPECT: INCLUDING SAME-SEX PARENTS

RATIONALE

A new book called *Making Room in the Circle: Lesbian, Gay, Bisexual and Transgender Families in Early Childhood Settings* (Lesser et al., 2005) makes it clear that early childhood educators must include all families, even ones they may not know much about. When any families are ignored, the message is strong and invites "silence, invisibility, secrecy, and shame" (Lesser et al., 2005). What does it mean to ignore families? It used to be that many families were ignored because classrooms mainly reflected white people of European roots—just as the history books teachers studied from in college told only white history—and only *male* white history at that. That area of ignorance began to be addressed back in the sixties and seventies. But today LGBT (lesbian, gay, bisexual, and transgender) families are only just beginning to be acknowledged in books and images aimed at early care and education programs and classrooms. According to Lesser, Burt, and Gelnaw, "Children's identities and sense of self are inextricably tied to their families. What happens when children never hear words nor see images that describe their families? . . . the message is clear: 'Your family is just not something to talk about'."

Gelnaw, Brickley, Marsh, and Ryan (2004) take this idea even further: "Silence is as powerful as what is said—or more. If children do not feel welcome to talk about their families at school, they are forced to leave a significant part of their lives behind when they enter the school or child care setting. This can have a negative impact on their self-esteem. When children do not feel comfortable in the school environment, their learning and development can be negatively affected."

It's not enough to just bring in books and images. Early childhood educators need to understand the kinds of conditions that affect LGBT families, which include political, legal, and socioeconomic ones. Furthermore, it's important to understand "the dangers that LGBT families face: loss of children, physical violence, danger to their homes and property, unstable employment, financial insecurity and rejections from their families of origin. As educators become aware of these conditions, the ethical responsibility to provide care and safety for children takes on new meaning" (Lesser et al., 2005).

It's also important to know that there are cultural differences in LGBT families and these may make their lives harder or easier. For example, some Native Americans believe in what are called two-spirit people. A two-spirit person has the gift of housing in the body both male and female spirits, which gives that person the ability to see the world from two perspectives.

The goal of your classroom or program should be to create an inclusive learning community where everyone feels safe and has a sense of belonging. Strategy 15 discusses how to do that through building relationships. Those approaches apply to programs that have LGBT families as well; in addition, consider the following approaches.

APPROACHES

- Recognize that family-centered programs provide the best education and support for children. To be family centered, early childhood professionals partner with all families, including LGBT ones.
- Create an environment of safety and trust. Confidentiality is an important part of such an environment.
- Create a welcoming environment that invites relationship building among *all* families and between families and teachers or staff.

- Unlearn any biases you have around sexual orientation and gender identity. Oppression is oppression, and you don't want to have any part of it—either supporting oppressive systems, practicing discrimination yourself, or harboring internal oppression.
- Learn the appropriate language related to LGBT families. Don't assume you know what anyone wants to be called; find out. The glossary in Lesser, Burt, and Gelnaw, pages 9–14, is almost sure to teach you something you don't know.
- Recognize that LGBT parents have struggles that most other parents don't have, such as asserting their right to exist as a family or keeping their family secret for the safety of their children. They also face a different set of legal issues around marriage, employment benefits, adoption, as well as divorce and child custody.
- Recognize that taking on challenges make you stronger. Struggling with your own religious beliefs and honoring *all* families at the same time may seem overwhelming. If the struggle isn't within you, you may find it among colleagues, between them and families, or among the families themselves. It may be hard to facilitate relationships with these struggles going on, but you have to do your best.
- A simple strategy for respecting all families is to check out your forms. Do they have spaces for the mother's name and the father's name or do they simply indicate parents' names?
- Watch out for events like Mother's Day and Father's Day when not all children have connections with a mother or a father. This issue doesn't just apply to LGBT families. Many children live in single-parent families with no connection to the other parent. How about skipping Mother's and Father's Days and just celebrating a Parents' Day?
- Address the family's strengths, not their weaknesses. Like all families, LGBT families have their unique strengths. In addition, they may have some strengths that are directly related to the challenges they face, such as the ability to express who they really are, willingness to take risks and move toward new forms and social structures, a deep desire and commitment to becoming a parent; as well as resilience and the ability to stand up to discrimination.

49 UNDERSTANDING AND APPRECIATING DIFFERENCES

RATIONALE

What do early care and education professionals (including family child care providers) do when parenting practices are questionable, yet the professional is trying to be culturally responsive and build a good relationship with the parent? How does he or she honor and respect diversity when parenting practices don't fit personal and professional definitions of good and right. How can teachers and providers respect and honor practices that seem to be incomprehensible, bad, wrong, or maybe even harmful?

If you haven't thought about diversity in terms of contradictions, this idea of honoring what seems wrong may confuse or upset you—put you off balance even. Those feelings are not bad—they can serve you well because when we enter a state of disequilibrium that's the perfect condition in which to learn something new. If we suspend judgment, understand that what looks wrong from our personal perspective, we can learn something by looking through someone else's eyes. It's uncomfortable to begin questioning what we already know, but it's important to do so when working in an early childhood setting with families you don't see eye to eye with.

Of course, causing harm to children is not something we can tolerate, but when we really begin to understand another's perspective, we may see that something that seems to hurt children doesn't when regarded in a different context.

A saying that clarifies this point comes from Dianna Ballesteros, a child care director who is a long-time advocate for the antibias movement in California. Dianna says, "En cada cabeza hay un mundo." "In each head there is a world." Expanding the world in one's own head is the means to understanding people who are different from one's self and goes way beyond just celebrating differences in ethnic foods, music, and customs. By acknowledging that each person has a different reality, you take the first step toward beginning to understand it.

But what about the diversity involving child-rearing practices that a teacher considers wrong? Take a family who sends a baby bottle in the lunch box for snack time for a kindergartener. As the teacher gets to know the mother, she realizes that the family is "babying" this child in more ways than one. "Babying" in her language has negative connotations. The mother and older siblings do everything for the child, which means she is often passive and seldom tries to do anything for herself, including putting on her own coat. When the kindergarten teacher talks to the preschool teacher, who has the same family in her program, she discovers that the mother is still spoon feeding the 4-year-old at home, even though both children feed themselves fine when no one is there to help them. The teachers worry to each other about these children's sense of independence—their self-esteem and their competence to take care of themselves. They agree that developing self-help skills is a major task of the early years. "Babying children" like that family is doing harms their sense of themselves as individuals!

The teachers are engaged in dualistic thinking, which makes it seem that if their ideas are right, the family has to be wrong. At the same time they want to be culturally responsive to the family, but they can't condone what the mother is doing. The teachers are coming from the context of Western culture and perspective, and they have the support of others who have the same kind of background, education, training, and experience. From their view this family's practice is known to cause harm. They even know the term for the type of harm—it's called codependence, and is what results in counseling when they grow up.

From another perspective neither of these practices is harmful and indeed, just the opposite. They are not only beneficial, but necessary in view of a particular set of goals. Edward Hall, anthropologist, in his book *Beyond Culture* uses an old saying about "apron strings" to explain differences. He writes, "The world can be divided into those cultures that prepare their children to be independent individuals and live apart from their family of origin as adults and those that do not. Those cultures that do not emphasize independence and individuality prepare their children to remain closely tied to the family as adults, living in close proximity if not in the same house, dwelling, or compound." In other words, one group cuts the apron strings and the other does not.

For many people trained in ECE, it is easy to see why cultures cut the apron strings and how they raise their children in preparation for the cutting. For those people it may be hard see the other view, and they may be extremely resistant to it. In theory, cultural differences can be very interesting; but practices are a different matter.

Families that don't cut the apron strings see independence and individuality as a threat not a goal. They are confident that their children will grow up to be independent, but they worry that they will be too independent and leave the family behind in their quest for individuality. So from birth on, the caregivers in these families dampen the flames of independence when they arise and instead teach the value of being dependent and of having others dependent on you.

The families who cut apron strings teach children self-help skills and encourage them to acknowledge the feat. "I did it all by myself" is not considered bragging, but an example of being proud of one's individual accomplishments. The families who are aiming at keeping bonds strong and families together downplay skills showing independence (which they figure are naturally built in and will arise no matter what). Instead of helping children take pride in individual accomplishments, they teach a skill that some would call "graciously accepting help."

Let's look a little closer at that notion of graciously accepting help. When a baby first starts trying to do things alone, that is when the lessons in graciously accepting help begin. These "lessons" may be entirely unconscious. People are so immersed in their culture that they don't think of why they are doing what they are doing, only that it feels right. If asked, they might say that they like doing things for their babies. Or maybe that their babies are too young to do things for themselves. They might not be able to explain that they are trying to keep their babies close to them and create strong lifelong ties. Most people have a hard time explaining their culture or how their actions and attitudes relate to it.

APPROACHES

- When something about a family's practices really bothers you, try to look at what they are doing through their eyes instead of your own.
- Try to withhold judgment long enough to gain a deeper understanding than first impressions allow.
- Don't just withhold judgment from people who are obviously from a different culture than yours. It may be easier for you to accept differences if you think the people have a valid cultural reason. But consider people who are of your culture who think differently from the way you do. Their reality is just as valid as someone who has a whole cultural way as a backup.
- Don't assume that doing things for children will make them grow up helpless and forever dependent. The modeling process is very strong. Children imitate what they see others doing. If one grows up seeing people helping others, they too become helpers in addition to receivers of help. Put that modeling effect together with a lifetime of lessons in respect for elders, you can see that it might result in the youngers helping the elders when the time comes that they need help.
- Just because the family who is doing what we disagree with is of the same culture as you are doesn't mean that they don't have their own reasons behind their practice. Work as hard to understand them as you do to understand families of cultures different from your own.
- See Strategy 21 for ideas about how to manage conflicts.

A story from the author: Teresa, who was from Mexico and a staff member in a program where I once worked, helped me see a perspective on meeting needs that was different from my perspective on the subject. I was telling her how important I thought it was for children to learn to meet their own needs as soon as possible. My argument usually went like this: If we meet our own needs, we are more able to help those who can't meet their needs. The flight attendants say in the plane, "In case of a loss of cabin pressure, put on your own oxygen mask before helping others." Behind that statement is the idea that if you lose consciousness, you won't be of any use to anybody else. Well, that's the way I was looking at the issue of meeting needs. We have to look out for ourselves first. I've never forgotten what Teresa said in response. "Janet, that's so sad. If you are looking out for yourself, that's only one person concerned about you. But if instead of focusing on yourself you think first of others, and if everybody else does the same, that's lots and lots of people looking out for you." That conversation stuck with me. It gave me a new way to think about things. I was able to see her point and honor our differences, but I didn't shift my whole frame of reference to become a person who no longer values independence and individuality. I am still who I am. I still have a particular set of values that relate to the way I was raised, my family of origin, and my culture, which I label as European American, white, Anglo or Celtic American, depending on to whom I am talking. I am who I am, but now have a broader perspective on differences.

50

WORKING WITH FAMILIES AROUND WHAT YOU BELIEVE ARE HARMFUL PRACTICES

RATIONALE

A difficult situation arises when the ECE professional finds out that what the family is doing is harmful to the child. If abuse or neglect is suspected, the professional must report it to the authorities. (See Strategy 40 on abuse and neglect.) If the behavior or practice doesn't fit the legal definition of abuse (which varies by state), it is a different matter. This is a delicate situation and must be handled sensitively. If you confront the family member with accusations, you may destroy the relationship that you have been building. If you ignore the situation, the child may suffer. Say, for instance, the grandmother enrolls her 3-month-old granddaughter and tells you that she is to be put to sleep on her stomach. When you hesitate, she insists that the baby can't sleep on her back and besides it's dangerous because she may spit up and choke. You think she is just old-fashioned or uninformed. But then she plays the cultural card and tells you that it is a tradition in her culture for babies to sleep on their tummies. Should you be culturally responsive and go along with her or will you argue that babies on their tummies are at risk for SIDS (Sudden Infant Death Syndrome)?

It will help both the baby and your relationship with the family if you seek to understand more about her ideas and cultural traditions. It's important to recognize that in some cultures SIDS is less of a risk than in others, especially if babies never sleep alone. Co-sleeping is common practice among many families. Also, regardless of culture, certain medical conditions put babies in more danger on their backs. That is not to say that you should automatically go along with what she says. You would be professionally remiss if you didn't share at least your understanding of the research that indicates babies are at greater risk for Sudden Infant Death Syndrome. Statistics may not impress her, but try to state things in terms she might listen to. Don't argue with her. Share your information in an open way and ask her more about her point of view. It might to help to find out if this is a common belief of her culture, or if some members (even if her family) have a different view of stomach sleeping. After all, it wasn't even a generation ago that everybody in the United States who followed medical advice placed their babies to sleep on their stomachs because it was considered safer than back sleeping.

A cultural practice that may startle teachers, caregivers, and providers is something called "coining," a healing or preventative practice of some people in various Asian cultures, which involves putting a special liquid on the skin and rubbing a coin or spoon on the area. The rubbing is hard enough to leave red marks and may appear to be an abusive practice unless you understand it.

One person's approved healing or preventative practice may seem abusive to someone who doesn't understand it. For example, think of immunization. If people had no idea about immunization, what would they think of a parent letting someone stick a needle in his baby's arm. The parent might explain to the doubters that this is a preventative measure and it doesn't harm the baby. But the observers may not believe it, especially if the baby cried in pain at the shot and especially if she got sick later on. Unless the observers were from a culture that believed in science and could accept the technical explanation of the procedure, they would have to take on faith that this was indeed a preventative measure, since they saw with their own eyes that it hurt the baby and made her ill. What would it take for someone who knew nothing about Western science or medicine to understand? What would it take for you to understand a healing or protection practice that was contradictory to Western science or medicine? We all need to be open to the idea that our way isn't the only right way.

APPROACHES

- Don't judge immediately. Seek to understand more. Barbara Rogoff (2003) suggests that even though judgments may be necessary, we can make better decisions when we do judge if we can move beyond the idea that our ideas are the only right ones. Only when we can see a situation in context and understand perspectives, ideas, and beliefs other than our own can we make wise judgments. (See Strategy 12 about conflicts and Strategy 20, Conflict Management.)
- At the same time you are not judging too quickly, don't hesitate to report abuse when it meets the legal definition of your state. Too often children die while the people who could have saved them held off on reporting suspected abuse.
- In all events, try to preserve whatever relationship you have managed to build with the family.
- Work on your listening skills. Using imagination helps too, as you try to see things from a perspective not your own. Try what Betty Jones and Renatta Cooper (2006) call "the believing game." They say, "Imagining another person's perspective on things requires the suspension of reality (what I really believe) in order to pretend. (This is what someone else believes. Could I, if I tried hard?) In the diverse world we live in, we keep encountering people who don't believe what we believe. We can sneer at them, or fight them, or pretend they're invisible (until they step on our toe). Or we can accept the challenge to 'embrace contraries'" (p. 23).
- Find people from diverse backgrounds with whom you can have discussions; then ask questions, and learn more.

References

Akbar, N. (1985). *The community of self*. Tallahassee, FL: Mind Productions.

American Psychological Association Online. (2004). *What is sexual orientation?* http://www.apa.org/pubinfo/answers.html

Baker, A. C., & Manfredi-Petitt, L. A. (1998). *Circle of love: Relationships between parents, providers and children in family child care*. St. Paul, MN: Redleaf Press.

Baker, Amy C., & Manfredi/Petitt, Lynn A. (2004). *Relationships, the heart of quality care: Creating community among adults in early care settings*. Washington, DC: National Association for the Education of Young Children.

Balaban, N. (2006). *Everyday goodbyes: Starting school and early care, a guide to the separation process*. New York: Teachers College Press.

Ballenger, C. (1992, Summer). Because you like us: The language of control. *Harvard Educational Review 62*(2),199–208.

Barrera, I., & Corso, R. (2003). *Skilled Dialogue*. Baltimore, MD: Brookes.

Bhavnagri, N., & Gonzalez-Mena, J. (1997, Fall). The cultural context of caregiving. *Childhood Education 74*(1), 2–8.

Bloom, P. J., Eisenberg, P., & Eisenberg, E. (2003, Spring/Summer). Reshaping early childhood programs to be more family responsive. *America's Family Support Magazine,* 36–38.

Brand, S. (1996, January). Making parent involvement a reality: Helping teachers develop partnerships with parents. *Young Children, 51*(2), 76–81.

Brault, L., & Brault, T. (2005). *Children with challenging behavior*. Phoenix, AZ: CPG Publishing.

Brault, L.M.V. (In Press). *Making inclusion work: Strategies to promote belonging for children with special needs in child care settings* Sacramento, CA: California Department of Education.

Bredekamp, S. (2003). Resolving contradictions between cultural practices. In C. Copple (Ed.), *A world of difference*. Washington, DC: National Association for the Education of Young Children.

Bredekamp, S., & Copple, C. (1997). *Developmentally appropriate early childhood programs* (2nd ed.). Washington, DC: National Association for the Education of Young Children.

Bruno, Holly Elissa. (2005, September). At the end of the day: Policies, procedures and practices to ensure smooth transitions. *Exchange, 165:* 66–69.

Caldwell, B. (2003). Advocacy is everybody's business. In B. Neugebauer & R. Neugebauer (Eds.), *The art of leadership*. Redmond, WA: Exchange Press.

Cannella, G. S. (1997). *Deconstructing early childhood education: Social justice and revolution*. New York: Peter Lang.

Carlson, V. J., & Hawwood, R. L. (1999–2000). Understanding and negotiating cultural differences concerning early developmental competence: The six raisin solution. *Zero to Three, 20*(3), 19–23.

Casper, V. (2003). Very young children in lesbian- and gay-headed families: Moving beyond acceptance. *Zero to Three, 23*(3), 18–26.

Chang, H. N., Muckelroy, A., & Pulido-Tobiassen, D. (1996). *Looking in, looking out: Redefining child care and education in a diverse society*. Oakland, CA: California Tomorrow.

Chao, R. (1994). Beyond parental control and authoritarian parenting style: Understanding Chinese parenting through the cultural notion of training. *Child Development, 65,* 1111–1119.

Children's Defense Fund. (2004). *The state of America's children*. Washington, DC.

Chodron, P. (2000). *When things fall apart*. Boston: Shambhala.

Clay, J. (1990). Working with lesbian and gay parents and their children. *Young Children, 45*(3), 31–35.

Clay, J. (2004). Creating safe, just places to learn for children of lesbian and gay parents: The NAEYC Code of Ethics in action. *Young Children, 59* (6), 34–38.

Covey, Stephan R. (2002). In Kerry Patterson, Joseph Grenny, Ron McMillan, & Al Switzler, *Crucial conversations*. New York: McGraw-Hill.

Curtis, D., & Carter, M. (2003). *Designs for living and learning*. St. Paul, MN: Redleaf Press.

Daniel, J. E. (1998, November). A modern mother's place is wherever her children are: Facilitating infant and toddler mothers' transitions in child care. *Young Children, 53*(6), 4–12.

Daper, L., & Duffy, B. (2001). Working with parents. In G. Pugh (Ed.), *Contemporary issues in the early years: Working collaboratively for children*. London: Paul Chapman Publishing.

DeLoache, J., & Gottlieb, A. (2000). *A world of babies: Imagined childcare guides for seven societies*. New York: Cambridge University Press.

Delpit, L. (1995). *Other people's children: Cultural conflict in the classroom*. New York: The New Press.

Derman-Sparks, L., & the Antibias Curriculum Task Force. (1989). *The anti-bias curriculum: Tools for empowering young children*. Washington, DC: National Association for the Education of Young Children.

Diffily, D. (2001, Summer). Family meetings: Teachers and families build relationships. *Dimensions of Early Childhood*, 5–9.

DiNatale, L. (2002, September). Developing high-quality family involvement programs in early childhood settings. *Young Children, 57*(5), 90–95.

Dombro, A. L., Colker, J., & Dodge, D. T. (1999). *The creative curriculum for infants and toddlers* (Rev. ed.). Washington, DC: Teaching Strategies.

Edelman, M. W. (2003, October 19). Children in America: A report card. Interview in *Parade Magazine*, p. 13.

Eggers-Pierola, C. (2005). *Connections and commitments: A Latino-based framework for early childhood educators*. Portsmouth, NH: Heinemann.

Epstein, J. L. (2001). *School, family, and community partnerships: Preparing educators and improving schools*. Boulder, CO: Westview.

Fasoli, L., & Gonzalez-Mena, J. (1997, March). Let's be real: Authenticity in child care. *Exchange, 150*, 35–40.

Fernandez, M. T., & Marfo, K. (2005). Enhancing infant-toddler adjustment during transitions to care. *Zero to Three, 26*, 41–48.

Fitzgerald, Damien. (2004). *Parent partnership in the early years*. London: Continuum.

Galinsky, E. (1998, March). Parents and teacher-caregivers: Sources of tension, sources of support. *Young Children, 43*(3), 4–12.

Garner, A. (2004). *Families like mine: Children of gay parents tell it like it is*. New York: HarperCollins Publishers.

Gartrell, D. (2004). *The power of guidance*. Washington, DC: National Association for the Education of Young Children.

Gelnaw, A., Brickley, M., Marsh, H., & Ryan, D. (2004). *Opening doors: Lesbian and gay parents and schools*. Washington, DC: Family Pride Coalition.

Gestwicki, Carol. (2004). *Home, school, and community relations: A guide to working with parents*. Albany, NY: Thompson Delmar.

Gonzalez-Mena, J. (1997, July). Cross cultural conferences. *Exchange, 116*, 55–58.

Gonzalez-Mena, J. (1997, September). Understanding the parent's perspective: independence or interdependence? *Exchange, 117*, 61–64.

Gonzalez-Mena, J. (1999, July). Dialogue to understanding across cultures. *Exchange, 128*, 6–8.

Gonzalez-Mena, J. (2002, January/February). Personal power: Creating new realities. *Child Care Information Exchange, 143*, 59–62.

Gonzalez-Mena, J. (2005a). *Diversity in early care and education: Honoring differences*. New York: McGraw-Hill.

Gonzalez-Mena, J. (2005b). *Foundations of early childhood education in a diverse society*. New York: McGraw-Hill.

Gonzalez-Mena, J. (2006). *The child in the family and the community* (4th ed.). Upper Saddle River, NJ: Merrill/Prentice Hall.

Gonzalez-Mena, J., & Bernhard, J. K. (1998, Summer). Out-of-home care of infants and toddlers: A call for cultural and linguistic continuity. *Interaction, 12*(2), 14–15.

Gonzalez-Mena, J., & Eyer, D. (2006). *Infants, toddlers, and caregivers*. New York: McGraw-Hill.

Gonzalez-Mena, J., & Shareef, I. (2005, November). Discussing diverse perspectives on guidance. *Young Children, 60*(6), 34–38.

Gonzalez-Mena, J., & Stonehouse, A. (2003, July/August). High-maintenance parent or parent partner? Working with a parent's concern. *Child Care Information Exchange*, 16–18.

Gordon, T. (2000). *Parent Effectiveness Training*. New York: Three Rivers Press.

Greenman, J. (1998, November/December). Parent partnerships: What they don't teach you can hurt. *Child Care Information Exchange*, 78–82.

Greenman, J. (2003). Places for childhood include parents too. In B. Neugebauer & R. Neugebauer (Eds.), *The art of leadership*. Redmond, WA: Exchange Press.

Greenman, J., & Stonehouse, A. (1996). *Prime times: A handbook for excellence in infant and toddler care*. St. Paul, MN: Redleaf Press.

Greenwood, P. M., & Cocking, R. R. (1994). *Cross-cultural roots of minority child development*. Hillsdale, NJ: Erlbaum.

Hale-Benson, J. (1986). *Black children: Their roots, culture and learning styles*. Baltimore, MD: Johns Hopkins University Press.

Hall, E. T. (1981). *Beyond culture*. Garden City, NY: Anchor Press/Doubleday.

Harkness, S., & Super, C. M. (Eds.). (1996). *Parents' cultural belief systems*. New York: Guilford Press.

Harwood, R. L., Miller, J. G., & Irizarry, N. L. (1995). *Culture and attachment: Perceptions of the child in context*. New York: Guilford Press.

Hooks, b. (2003). *Rock my soul: Black people and self-esteem*. New York: Atria.

Jacobson, T. (2003). *Confronting our discomfort: Clearing the way for anti-bias in early childhood*. Portsmouth, NH: Heinemann.

Jones, E., & Cooper, R. (2006). *Playing to get smart*. New York: Teachers College Press.

Kagiticibasi, C. (1996). *Family and human development across cultures*. Mahwah, NJ: Erlbaum.

Kaiser, Barbara, & Rasminsky, Judy S. (2003). *Challenging behavior in young children: Understanding, preventing, and responding effectively*. Boston: Allyn and Bacon.

Katz, L. (1977). *Talks with teachers: Reflections on early childhood education*. Washington, DC: National Association for the Education of Young Children.

Katz, L. (1996). Child development knowledge and teacher preparation: Confronting assumptions. *Early Childhood Research Quarterly, 11*(2), 135–146.

Keyser, J. (2001). Creating partnerships with families: Problem-solving through communication. *Child Care Information Exchange* (138), 4–7.

Kitayama, S., Markus, H., & Matsumoto. (1995). Culture, self, and emotion: A cultural perspective on "self-conscious" emotions. In J. P. Tangeny & K. W. Fischer (Eds.), *Self-conscious emotions: The psychology of shame, guilt, embarrassment, and pride*. New York: Guilford Press.

Kreidler, W. J., & Whitall, S. (2003). Resolving conflict. In C. Copple (Ed.), *A world of difference: Readings on teaching children in a diverse society*, (pp. 52–56). Washington, DC: National Association for the Education of Young Children.

Lakey, Jennifer. (1997, May). Teachers and parents define diversity in an Oregon preschool cooperative —Democracy at work. *Young Children: 52*(4), 20–26.

Lally, J. R. (1995, November). The impact of child care policies and practices on infant-toddler identity formation. *Young Children,* 58–67.

Lane, M., & Signer, S. (1990). *A guide to creating partnerships with parents*. Sacramento, CA: California Department of Education and WestEd.

Lee, L. (2004). *Stronger together: Family support and early childhood education*. San Rafael, CA: Parent Services Project.

Lee, L., & Seiderman, E. (1998). *Families matter: The Parent Services Project*, Cambridge, MA: Harvard Family Research Project.

Lesser, L. K., Burt, T., & Glenaw, A. (2005). *Making Room in the Circle: Lesbian, Gay, Bisexual and Transgender Families in Early Childhood Settings*. San Rafael, CA: Parent Services Project.

Levine, J. A. (1993a). *Getting men involved: Strategies for early childhood programs*. New York: Scholastic.

Levine, J. A. (1993b). Involving fathers in Head Start: A framework for public policy and program development. *Families in Society, 74*(1), 4–19.

Lewis, C. C. (1995). *Educating hearts and minds: Reflections on Japanese preschool and elementary education*. New York: Cambridge University Press.

Lewis, E. G. (1996). What Mother? What Father? *Young Children 51*(3), 27.

Lieberman, A. (1995). Concerns of immigrant families. In P. Mangione (Ed.), *A guide to culturally*

sensitive care, (pp. 28–37). Sacramento, CA: California Department of Education and WestEd.

Lin, C. Y., & Fu, V. (1990). A comparison of child-rearing practices among Chinese, immigrant Chinese, and Caucasian-American parents. *Child Development, 61,* 429–433.

Link, G., & Beggs, M. with Seiderman, E. (1997). *Serving families*. Fairfax, CA: Parent Services Project.

Lopez, E. J., Salas, L., & Flores, J. P. (2005, November). Hispanic preschool children: What about assessment and intervention? *Young Children, 60*(6), 48–54.

Lubeck, S. (1996). Deconstructing "child development knowledge" and "teacher preparation." *Early Childhood Research Quarterly, 11*(2):147–168.

Mangione, P. (Ed.). (1995). *A guide to culturally sensitive care*. Sacramento, CA: California Department of Education and WestEd.

Meisels, S. J., & Atkins-Burnett, S. (2005). *Developmental screening in early childhood*. Washington, DC: National Association for the Education of Young Children.

Miller, Karen. (2005). *Simple transitions for infants and toddlers*. Beltsville, MD: Gryphon House.

Modigliani, Kathy. (1997). *Parents speak about child care*. Boston: Wheelock College Family Child Care Project.

New, R. S. (1999, March). Here, we call it "drop off and pickup": Transition to child care, American style. *Young Children, 54*(2), 34–35.

Nyman, S. I. (2003). Mentoring advocates in the context of early childhood education. In B. Neugebauer & R. Neugebauer (Eds.), *The art of leadership*. Redmond, WA: Exchange Press.

Palmer, P. (1997). *The courage to teach*. San Francisco: Jossey Bass.

Parent Services Project (PSP). (2001). *Working together for children and families* [Brochure]. San Rafael, CA: Author.

Parlakian, R. (2001). *The power of question: Building quality relationships with families* [Brochure]. Washington, DC: Zero to Three.

Phillips, C., & Cooper, R. (1992). Cultural dimensions of feeding relationships. *Zero to Three, 12*(6), 10–13.

Phillips, C. B. (1995). Culture, a process that empowers. In P. Mangione (Ed.), *A guide to culturally sensitive care* pp. 2–9. Sacramento, CA: California Department of Education and WestEd.

Pope, J., & Seiderman, E. (2001, Winter). The child-care connection. *Family Support, 19*(4), 24–35.

Ratekin, C., & Bess, G. (2003). Making the partnership stronger—Working with a board of directors. In B. Neugebauer & R. Neugebauer (Eds.), *The art of leadership*. Redmond, WA: Exchange Press.

Robinson, A., & Stark, D. R. (2002). *Advocates in action: Making a difference for young children*. Washington, DC: National Association for the Education of Young Children.

Rogoff, B. (1990). *Apprenticeship in thinking*. New York: Oxford University Press.

Rogoff, B. (2003). *The cultural nature of human development*. New York: Oxford University Press.

Rothstein-Fisch, C. (2003). *Bridging cultures: Teacher education module*. Mahwah, NJ: Erlbaum.

Russell, G. M. (2004). Surviving and thriving in the midst of anti-gay politics. *The Policy Journal of the Institute for Gay and Lesbian Strategic Studies, 7*(20): 1–7.

Seiderman, E. (1997 January). Parent/staff partnerships. *Child Care Information Exchange, 113*, 47–49.

Seiderman, E. (2003). Putting all the players on the same page: Accessing resources for the child and family. In B. Neugebauer & R. Neugebauer (Eds.), *The art of leadership*. Redmond, WA: Exchange Press.

Small, M. (1998). *Our babies, ourselves: How biology and culture shape the way we parent*. New York: Anchor Books.

Sullivan, D. (2003). *Learning to lead*. St. Paul, MN: Redleaf Press.

Thaxton, S. M. (2003). Grandparents as parents: Understanding the issues. In B. Neugebauer & R. Neugebauer (Eds.), *The art of leadership*. Redmond, WA: Exchange Press.

Tobaissen, D. P., & Gonzalez-Mena, J. (1998). *A place to begin: Working with parents on issues of diversity*. Oakland, CA: California Tomorrow.

Triandis, H. C. (1989). Cross-cultural studies of individualism and collectivism. *Nebraska Symposium on Motivation, 37*, 43–133.

Turnbull, A., & Turnbull, R. (2001). *Families, professionals, and exceptionality: Collaborating for empowerment* (4th ed.). Upper Saddle River, NJ: Merrill/Prentice Hall.

Trumbull, E., Diaz-Meza, R., Hasan, A., & Rothstein-Fisch, C. (2001). *Five-year report of the Bridging Cultures Project: 1996–2000*. San Francisco: WestEd. http://www.WestEd.org/BridgingCultures

Trumbull, E., & Farr, B. (2005). *Language and learning: What teachers need to know*. Norwood, MA: Christopher-Gordon.

Unell, B. C., & Wyckoff, J. L. (2000). *The eight seasons of parenthood. How the stages of parenting constantly reshape our adult identities*. New York: Time Books.

Uttal, L. (2002). *Making care work: Employed mothers in the new childcare market*. New Brunswick, NJ: Rutgers University Press.

Whiting, B. B., & Edwards, C. P. (1998). *Children of different worlds: The formation of social behavior*. Cambridge, MA: Harvard University Press.

Zepeda, M., Gonzalez-Mena, J., Rothstein-Fisch, C., & Trumbull, E. (2006). *Bridging cultures in early care and education: A Training Module*. Mahwah, NJ: Erlbaum.

Index

Abuse
  emotional, families referred for, 100
  families referred for, 100–101, 101f
  physical, families referred for, 100
  sexual, families referred for, 100
Active listening, 103
Adult behaviors, authority-related, 20–21
Advisory boards, parents' roles in, 56–57, 57f
Advocacy
  parents becoming advocates for all
    children, 3–4
  parents as advocates for their own
    children, 1–2, 2f
  parents concerned about school
    readiness, 5–7, 6f
Antibias, defined, 8
Antibias Curriculum Task Force, 8
Antibias Curriculum, The, 8
Antibias environment, 8–10, 9f, 10f
Assessment, 11–13, 12f, 13f
Attachment, 14–16, 16f
Attitude(s), of professionals, 17–19, 18f
Authority
  adult behaviors related to, 20–21
  teacher *vs.* parent, 22–23

Ballenger, Cynthia, 20
Ballesteros, Dianna, 120
Barrera, Isaura, 50
Bay Area Male Involvement Network, 68–69
Behavior(s)
  adult, authority-related, 20–21
  nonverbal, 34
Behavior changes, parent
    discussion of, 24–25
Beyond Cultures, 121
Bias, of early childhood professionals,
    17–19, 18f
Blind spot, 50
Bombeck, Erma, 2
Bredekamp, S., 50
Brickley, M., 118
*Bridging Cultures in Early Care and
    Education*, 30

Broadway Children's School, 80f
Burt, T., 119

Care
  culturally responsive, 54–55
  education and, link between, 26–29,
    27f, 28f
  educational practices and, conflicts
    between, 30–31
Caregiver(s)
  concerns of, talking with families
    about, 108–109
  helping parents help child entering
    program, 110–112, 111f
*Caring Spaces, Learning Places: Children's
    Environments That Work*, 26
Challenge to Care in Schools, The, 27
Child advocacy. *See* Advocacy
Children
  abuse or neglect of, families referred for,
    100–101, 101f
  separation from family, adjustment to,
    96–97, 97f
  with special needs, families of, 81–82
Children's Defense Funds, 3, 40
Classroom, parents in, 91–93, 92f, 93f
Collectivism, 30
Communication
  environments for, 60–61, 61f
  nonverbal, across cultures, 34–35, 35f
  through writing, 34–36, 34f–36f
Community
  creating sense of, 37–39, 38f, 39f
  defined, 37
Community resources, referrals for,
    40–42, 42f
Competition, between parents and
    professional, 42–43, 43f
Complaint(s), of parents, working with,
    86–87
Concerns, of teachers and caregivers,
    talking with families about,
    108–109
"Concerns of Immigrant Families," 78